Emily & Shawn,

ATHEIST DOCTOR TO PALM BEACH MINISTER

Jesus is Lord!

God Bless.

ATHEIST DOCTOR TO PALM BEACH MINISTER

Rev. Dwight M. Stevens, M.D., Th.D.

Front and back cover author photographs by Kate Kuhner
Back cover Paramount photograph by Cal Landau
Cover Logo by Gil Lavelanet
Cover design by 99Designs
Edited by Michele Dargan, Michele Dargan Media
Printed by CreateSpace

Library of Congress Control Number: 2016917535
CreateSpace Independent Publishing Platform
North Charleston, South Carolina

ISBN-13: 9781539598206
ISBN-10: 1539598209

Audiobook in production.

FIRST EDITION: February 2017

Facebook: ATHEIST DOCTOR TO PALM BEACH MINISTER
www.paramountchurchpb.com
www.missionsofmercyfl.org
paramountchurchpb@gmail.com

Printed in the United States of America

Acknowledgments

THE IDEA TO WRITE THIS BOOK BEGAN TEN YEARS AGO, WHEN HOWARD MINSKY, THE producer of the film *Love Story,* first gave me the inspiration. Howard was in the audience on November 7, 2002 when we began a classic movie series at the Paramount Church with the showing of the silent film *Beau Geste.* It was the first film ever shown at the Palm Beach Paramount Theater on January 9, 1927. The classic film series has continued monthly as a community service ever since.

Howard became our advisor on what films to show. He became a special friend as he began to attend and enjoy our church services. His book, *The Love of My Life,* is his story. He repeatedly encouraged me to tell *my story,* culminating in this book.

Once this project began, many friends encouraged me with their thoughts, comments, suggestions, corrections and gracious review of chapters. These include:

Maria Bacinich

Bill Benson

Bob Boutwell

Kate Kuhner Broda

Phillip Causey

Candice Cohen

Rosa Corley

Tom Dibiasi

Rev. John & Ruth Genco

Raphael Giglio

Rev. Joseph Guadagnino

Lou Hamby

Elizabeth Hoadley

Lelah Jackson

Gil Lavelanet

Dr. Arthur Lebowitz

Rosana Levin

Jean O'Brien

Dr. Bill Quayle

Dr. Michael Reed

Warren Steffens

Peter Stephens

Craig Stevens

Don Stevens

Win Stevens, my brother

Bruce Taylor

Vicki

I also wish to acknowledge and give special thanks to the physicians, dentists and ministers who have accompanied me on my twenty-nine medical/dental/ministry/construction mission trips since 1988.

Physicians

Dr. Sandy Carden, Internist & Infectious Disease Specialist

Dr. Jon Fierer, Internist

Dr. John Murray, Otolaryngologist

Dr. Bill Quayle, Ophthalmologist

Dr. Jana Rasmussen, Plastic Surgeon

Dr. Michael Reed, Dermatologist

Dr. Bob Swisher, Gastroenterologist

Dr. Graham Whitfield, Orthopedic Surgeon

Dentists

Dr. Pearl Burns

Dr. Karl Foose

Dr. Bruce Holz

Dr. Mark Kuhl

Dr. Eric Lowenhaupt

Dr. Arnold Rothman

Dr. Luis Sarria

Dr. Dale Smith

Ministers

Rev. John Genco

Rev. Joseph and Bea Guadagnino

Rev. Tony Guadagnino

Rev. Joe and Mary Overall Rich

My appreciation goes to CreateSpace for their guidance and assistance through the publication process.

Photographs of my aunt Inez playing the accordion and great Uncle Victor also playing the accordion provided by my cousin Margo L. Clonts.

And a very special thanks to Michele Dargan, a journalist for 28 years who spent the last 20 years at the *Palm Bach Daily News*. She retired in April 2016 and founded Michele Dargan Media, a writing, editing and public relations company. Michele meticulously edited the entire book in preparation for printing.

Lastly, I must acknowledge that I had help in writing this book.

Beginning in March 2015, I started writing thoughts, which became chapters, which became a massive unwieldy assemblage of 100-110 chapters. I can only describe it as train-of-thought.

Planting this four-inch thick notebook in front of an accomplished author and friend, Elizabeth Hoadley, resulted in a dramatic recoiling shriek of disbelief.

Rightly so.

Anything and everything was included.

To the tune of over five hundred pages.

Over thirty chapters were on theological subjects, from lengthy explanations of ten Old Testament passages to dissertations on the Books of Psalms AND Proverbs.

With a carving knife, chapters after chapters were whittled away and the remaining chapters reworked into something *maybe interesting.*

Night after night when no inspiration came, I would fall asleep with nothing in my mind to write, only to awaken around 3 a.m. each night with fresh thoughts and flying fingers on the keyboard for the next one to two hours.

If there is anything inspirational in the following pages, it can only be attributed to God and His grace, the inspiration of the Holy Spirit and an understanding of my Lord and Savior Jesus Christ.

To THEM ... be all glory and praise!

TABLE OF CONTENTS

INTRODUCTION

I WAS AN ATHEIST.

There was no God!

I was, and still am a medical doctor with an active medical license.

I became a pastor … of a church … in Palm Beach.

How did an atheist medical doctor become a pastor of a church in Palm Beach?

This book answers that question.

It is a question that has been posed to me more times than I can count.

It is not a simple story. It is a long, convoluted story that began by being born to a provincial Italian Mother and an English father, whom I never knew. The story winds through the suburbs of St. Louis, to a New Year's Eve party in San Diego, to London, England, to the hallowed halls of New York University, to the French Riviera and finally lands in an historic movie theater in Palm Beach.

The tale is unvarnished, with admissions of heartbreak, a car crash in Kansas, reluctant jazz dancing in Greenwich Village, pursuit of an LPGA Open champion and medical missions to the Andes Mountains of South America.

Everything culminated in a spiritual awakening in the early morning hours of June 1, 1985.

The merciful hand of God touched my life, the response to the prayers of some patients from my dermatology practice.

Thirty-one years later, an unshakeable belief in God and in the Gospel of Jesus Christ has molded me into who I am today.

This book is not intended to be a book of theology. There are chapters about Jesus, the Gospel of Jesus Christ, the Four Gospels, even a chapter on the Book of Revelation. But this is not an exhaustive or comprehensive attempt to explain the Bible.

It is just my story.

Maybe it will be the catalyst for someone to believe in God and in the Gospel of Jesus Christ.

Rev. Dwight M. Stevens, M.D., Th.D.

CHAPTER

1

Palm Beach, Florida

HIS INFLUENCE WAS UNPARALLELED IN PALM BEACH.

I sat across from this eminently distinguished attorney, in his more-than-impressive office, circled by photographs of people most of us only see on TV. All Republicans, of course.

This was Palm Beach "Old Guard." Not a smattering of nouveau.

On his desk was a plaque with his trademark saying: *"Be Reasonable, Do It My Way."*

Well known as a great negotiator, it was predictable that the end of his consultations inevitably resulted with the other side always seeing it *his way.*

But then, he did know best. The awards, too numerous to count from both local and state organizations, testified to this.

His office walls told their own stories about the character and likes of this man. A stuffed 20-inch permit and a 25-inch bonefish were prominently displayed. Permit, a Western Atlantic Ocean game fish, are notoriously strong fighters, so much so that the U.S. Navy named two of its submarines *USS Permit*. Doyle probably landed this fish after an endurance contest, with Doyle being stronger and more stubborn to outlast this prize. The bonefish was likely from one his coveted sport-fishing getaways to the nearby Bahamas.

He was dressed impeccably, as always.

He wore a gray pinstripe suit, probably Brooks Brothers or Maus & Hoffman, a pressed white, button-down shirt … all were set off by the ubiquitous Palm Beach Hermés tie, probably a gift from one of his adoring, elite clients.

I also dressed well. I learned that from my four years of living in Manhattan, where a more seasoned New Yorker friend introduced me to Barneys.

But none of that was the topic of today's appointment and it certainly wouldn't influence his response to my outlandish, soon-to-be-spilled-out, request. Palm Beach was full of external facades that masked internal nefarious intentions.

He knew that.

I knew that.

He was far too smart and too experienced to be influenced by someone else's Brooks Brothers or Maus & Hoffman suit.

In the spring of 1992, upon learning of my impending retirement from private practice, we slowly walked out of my office together. He said, "If I can help you in any way, let me know." A very gracious and sincere statement that was typical of Doyle.

At the time, I had no idea that a little more than a year later, I would be sitting in his office taking him up on his offer.

I was about to ask for his help in launching a project never accomplished in Palm Beach since 1926.

To say I was armed with an offer he couldn't refuse would be ludicrous.

But I did have three things going for me, I hoped.

First, was our previous professional relationship that had evolved into a friendship.

Second, was that he had mentioned to me several times that both his father and one of his brothers were named "Dwight." That may not sound like a big deal, but to this day I have never ever met another person named Dwight. I just haven't. I've read about a few Dwights. But not once have I met one. Maybe Doyle had experienced the same.

Third, was my *portfolio,* a one-inch thick white binder from Office Depot containing my months of research for this church project.

The truth was, and I knew it, that none of those reasons were sufficient to convince this tower of influence to represent me before the Palm Beach Town Council.

Even my call to make the appointment was met with some mild resistance, but I managed to convince his secretary that I needed his legal services.

I sat there silently praying, as I had been for weeks, in nervous anticipation of this make-or-break meeting.

I hoped I was not fidgeting too noticeably.

I couldn't just sit there facing him. I had to speak.

I thought, *"Here goes. Let's see if this really is God's plan."*

2

"DOYLE, I WOULD LIKE TO START A CHURCH IN THE PARAMOUNT AND I'D LIKE YOU TO represent us before the Town Council."

After I had somehow found the courage to sputter it out, the silence that followed was palpable.

What a statement!

To him, I was no doubt still a dermatologist, recently retired from private practice.

Yes, I had become an ordained minister and had also obtained a doctorate in theology, but Doyle certainly didn't know that yet.

Maybe he knew of the four medical mission trips I had taken since 1988.

But start a church?

In Palm Beach?

This had to sound more than a little unrealistic to a man who *was* Palm Beach.

No doubt he had heard many proposals from far more accomplished and polished entrepreneurs. It was evident he was trying to come up with a kind and diplomatic way of saying, "No."

I was now intently looking for the non-verbal signs of communication … the body language, the facial expression, the tone and the inflection of his words.

His facial expression gave away nothing. He was too good at this to provide "tells" to anyone in negotiations.

And although his body language wasn't overt, he stiffened just a little bit as he kept eye contact with me. He was evidently thinking how to respond.

What came out of his kind, soft and genuinely sincere voice was "Well, I'm not sure that's such a good idea," he said with just a touch of a Southern Georgia accent.

And though he didn't frown or furrow his brow, he wasn't exactly smiling either.

He continued to keep eye contact.

This was going to be easy for him to decline.

I had anticipated that at first he would be reluctant. But I had erroneously assumed he would at least ask me why I was even considering the idea.

Instead he was saying the equivalent of a very diplomatic, "No."

Another Palm Beach attorney now deceased, Paul Williams, had commented to me several years earlier, after a memorial service at the Royal Poinciana Chapel in which we both gave eulogies, "You should have been a trial attorney." I wondered at the time, "Was he that impressed with my public speaking ability?"

I now had to bring that to the table with Doyle.

Present the evidence.

Make my case to a man who picked his clients.

I had to convince Doyle Rogers, one of Palm Beach's most respected and influential attorneys, to represent me.

If only I could preface my presentation with a summary of the last eight years of my life and how I became a believer in God and Jesus Christ after being a life-long atheist …

And tell him of my journeys through college and medical school and the many nudges from God that led me to a New York University internship and residency in dermatology and to my private practice with the Palm Beach Medical Group just across the north bridge.

If only I could tell him of the doors that miraculously opened to obtain a lease at the Paramount, with the encouragement of H. Loy Anderson Jr., Jim Partington and the Palm Beach Civic Association.

And tell him of the lease we had agreed upon for the church at the Paramount, which was never co-signed by the Resolution Trust Corporation …

And tell him about the twenty-six times I was told "No" for possible locations in Palm Beach - until *THE CALL CAME* …

And tell him about Gene Lawrence, the most notable commercial architect in Palm Beach in the last thirty years, who was voluntarily going to design the church.

I took a slow, deep breath, hoping not to be too obvious in doing so, and started talking. I tried to hit the highlights, knowing I had to do the whole presentation in about two minutes.

"I know it sounds a little unusual, but I'd like to explain why I am considering this," I said.

Not a bad start, I thought.

I didn't stutter.

I wasn't too tongue-tied.

I wasn't sweating.

Keep it up.

He was listening. Or at least pretending to listen.

Maybe it was because his father was named "Dwight" and one of his brothers was also named "Dwight."

I had to present some facts … fast.

Where to start?

How about the last eight years that had changed the course of my life?

How do I tell him that I hadn't believed in God because of my experiences growing up?

I didn't even know there was an Old Testament and a New Testament.

That all changed on June 1, 1985.

I later became an ordained minister, had obtained a doctorate degree in theology and began leading a weekly bible study in the Palm Beach Civic Association board room.

Would he understand?

How could he?

It all now hinged on *"The Portfolio."*

It was time to whip out my one-inch thick white binder from Office Depot with the cover title *"PALM BEACH CHRISTIAN CHURCH,"* above which was a delicate four-pointed cross.

I handed it to him.

CHAPTER

3

Eilat, Israel

"YOU KNOW WE WERE PRAYING FOR YOU," MUFFY SAID.

It was the spring of 2000 and we were sitting at an outside café in Eilat, Israel, overlooking the Red Sea. Muffy Brooks and her husband, Bill, were touring Israel as part of our group of eighteen from the Palm Beach Fellowship of Christians & Jews.

Her comment stunned me.

It also gave me a vital piece of a mystifying puzzle that began for me on June 1, 1985.

Prior to that date I had accomplished a lot.

I graduated from Washington University in St. Louis with a B.A. in Biology.

I had received an M.D. from Missouri University Medical School, where I also taught anatomy for two years.

My medical school offered elective periods during the third and fourth years in which students could select specific areas of interest in medicine. I did six of those: three in dermatology at New York University, Massachusetts General Hospital and St. John's Institute for Diseases of the Skin in London; one in general surgery and one in plastic surgery in San Diego and one in Cardiology at M.D. Anderson in Houston.

I completed a four-year internship and residency in dermatology at the world-renowned New York University Skin & Cancer Unit in Manhattan.

For the past eight years, I practiced dermatology with the respected Palm Beach Medical Group on 7th Street and Olive Avenue, just across the Flagler Memorial Bridge connecting Palm Beach to West Palm Beach.

I had been engaged to be married and subsequently unengaged.

I was a well-educated and somewhat urbane 38-year-old.

And I was a fool.

Psalms 14:1 and 53:1 say: "The fool says in his heart, 'There is no God.'"

That was me.

June 1, 1985 changed that dramatically.

Within a few months, I enrolled in a Bible college and subsequently obtained a master's and a doctorate in theology.

I began taking medical mission trips to developing countries.

In 1992, I retired from a very successful and lucrative private practice of dermatology after fifteen years and offered my medical services as a dermatologist with the Palm Beach County Health Department for the next twelve years.

I started a Bible study in my home in North Palm Beach.

This circuitous path led me to that appointment in the cloistered office of my former patient and Palm Beach attorney Doyle Rogers.

And now Muffy was providing the elusive piece to the puzzle of how I was taken from a total non-belief in God … non-belief in the Bible … non-belief in Jesus Christ … zero church attendance … to an absolute belief in God … an invitation of Jesus Christ into my heart … and a belief that I was called to become a pastor and founder of a church in Palm Beach.

So it all began with Janet Rich, I thought. *Could she have started all this?*

Sometime before June 1, 1985, a delightful woman named Janet Rich was a patient in my dermatology practice. Her husband, Bob, was the founder and owner of Rich Products. The company was sponsor and namesake of Rich Stadium, home of the Buffalo Bills football team. Bob also owned Palm Beach National Golf Club. Janet had invited me on several occasions to play golf there.

More importantly, I shockingly discovered that she, along with some other ladies from Palm Beach including Muffy Brooks and Connie Miesel, were in the habit of meeting every week to pray for people.

I was on their list.

Somehow, through her visits to me as a patient and our talks on the clubhouse terrace at Palm Beach National after a round of golf, Janet discovered that I didn't believe in God or Jesus.

She brought my name before that group and they prayed for me to become a believer in God and Jesus Christ.

God waited for the perfect time to get my attention and answer their prayers.

That fateful day was June 1, 1985.

But the stage was already being set at Frenchman's Creek Golf Course in 1983.

CHAPTER

4

Frenchman's Creek, Palm Beach Gardens, Florida

"I'VE TURNED MY LIFE OVER TO GOD," BILL SAID.

I didn't know what to say to that.

I never heard of such a thing nor had anyone ever uttered something so seemingly preposterous. But there I sat, in the office of my best friend Bill Hobbs, head golf pro at Frenchman's Creek in North Palm Beach.

It was January 3, 1983.

At that time, there were two eighteen-hole golf courses at Frenchman's Creek in addition to a small restaurant and an even smaller pro shop. No homes were built on what would later become an elite, private residential development with access for yachts to the Intracoastal Waterway.

But in 1983, it was the place to be if one loved golf, which I did and still do.

A typical day at Frenchman's Creek found Jack Nicklaus - already winner of seventeen major championships - practicing with his teacher, Jack Grout, while caddy, Angelo, shagged balls. Then Nicklaus would jaunt off to the practice green for some short-game practice with Phil Rodgers.

Jack Wullkotte, Nicklaus' personal club maker and future Hall of Fame club maker, was always nearby. This unequalled craftsman became a friend and personal club maker for me.

Imagine that!

Jack Nicklaus' personal club maker would invite me to his shop, the not-open-to-the-public "Bear's Lair," to make custom golf clubs for me!

It was heady stuff!

Also on the range were Jim Flick, Tony Pena and Gardner Dickenson, along with several of the LPGA professionals including Judy Clark, soon to become Judy Dickenson.

It was a great place to become saturated in the world of professional golf and I loved being there. My home was nearby and Frenchman's was the perfect place for me.

I played a lot of golf, but it had all been self-taught. Consistency eluded me. Maybe Bill could help. And he did, patiently teaching me the basics of the golf swing and of the short game.

And we became friends.

We were both single at the time and enjoyed both the golf atmosphere and the abundance of women golfers. It was a golf-loving bachelor's paradise.

But his out-of-the-blue comment, *"I've turned my life over to God,"* threw me.

I didn't know what to say. So I didn't say anything.

I sat there silently, *thinking,* "Bill, have I got a therapist for you!"

Soon afterwards, Bill was offered a plum position at Harbour Town Golf Club on Hilton Head Island. As he left town, the topic of God never came up again. I later learned that the previous day, one of the LPGA touring pros, Julie Cole, had shared her belief and faith in Jesus Christ with Bill. That led to him inviting Christ into his life and turning his life over to God.

And I was the first person he told.

My response couldn't have been too encouraging.

Nevertheless, Bill would soon embark on a path that led him to leave the world of professional golf and begin working with Youth for Christ in Palm Beach County. Eventually, he founded Urban Youth Impact, an extensive inner-city outreach to at-risk youth in West Palm Beach.

Little did I know that Bill's out-of-the-blue comment about *"turning his life over to God"* would stick in the recesses of my mind. God was nudging me and calling me, but I didn't know it at the time.

Two-and-a-half years later, it all surfaced like an unexpected volcanic explosion that permanently changed the landscape and course of my life.

CHAPTER

5

Delray Beach, Florida

SHE WAS A COMBINATION OF FARAH FAWCETT AND SUSAN ANTON.

That's how I described Vicki.

We had been engaged to be married for about six months. She was the most wonderful woman in the world and, without a doubt, the absolute "love of my life."

My dream girl.

Gorgeous.

Outwardly, she looked like God had combined the stunning physical features of Farrah Fawcett and Susan Anton.

Personable, sociable, fashionable, energetic, funny, never met a stranger and a *great dancer!*

But Vicki had called off the engagement two months earlier.

I was heartbroken.

Why did she break off our engagement?

Even today it isn't totally clear to me. But I'm sure it had much to do with my arrogant, selfish, critical, condescending and argumentative manner in those days.

I was well-educated and very successful in my profession. But, to be honest, I was a bit of a pain at times to be around.

After she broke off our engagement, Vicki would not see me or even talk with me.

Nothing!

It was so painful, so heartbreakingly painful, that I sought ways to make the pain go away - a few beers, a marijuana joint, psychotherapy counseling, the companionship of other women.

Nothing worked.

Until it happened!

CHAPTER
6

North Palm Beach, Florida

"THIS PAIN WILL NEVER GO AWAY UNTIL YOU TURN YOUR LIFE OVER TO GOD."

It was June 1, 1985, 4 a.m.

I was abruptly awakened from a deep sleep and sat up in bed, with this startling thought in my mind:

> *"This pain will never go away until you turn your life over to God."*

Bill Hobbs had expressed that same phrase to me two-and-a-half years earlier. *"Turn your life over to God."*

Now somehow, inexplicably and emphatically, *that same thought was in my mind at that moment!*

We have all heard of people who only believe in God because of some crisis, some emotional upheaval or some cataclysmic trauma. Usually the individual is dismissed as someone who clutched onto God because they couldn't handle life's trials. That certainly was my attitude.

I did have an emotional upheaval that preceded being awakened at 4 a.m.

This middle-of-the-night awakening occurred when I was experiencing the unrelenting heartbreak of a broken engagement. Nevertheless, this foreign thought caught my attention.

Big time!

The impact of the thought, *"This pain will never go away until you turn your life over to God,"* was enormous.

First, this specific thought was absolutely foreign to me. And this thought was counter to my whole belief system about God.

I didn't believe in God!

And I had absolutely no clue what it meant to *"turn one's life over to God."*

How in the world did one *"turn one's life over to God?"*

It wasn't an audible voice.

There wasn't an angel sitting on the side of the bed.

It was a thought implanted in my mind.

From where?

Ten years later, I learned that it was the direct result of the prayers of Muffy Brooks, Janet Rich and Connie Miesel.

As I lay there wondering what this meant and where this thought came from, I recalled that two-and-a-half years earlier Bill Hobbs had used the same exact phrase. He told me that he had *"turned his life over to God."*

At that time, I thought he needed a therapist.

Now I needed to talk to Bill.

I called him.

CHAPTER

7

WHAT DOES IT MEAN TO "TURN ONE'S LIFE OVER TO GOD?"

Hopefully Bill could answer that for me.

He had recently come back to the area and was now head golf pro at PGA National in Palm Beach Gardens. I mumbled something about needing to talk to him about God. He graciously invited me to dinner with him and his wife that evening, a Saturday, which I thankfully accepted.

That evening we talked over dinner. But I don't recall understanding much of what he said. He invited me to accompany him to church the next day and I went with him to Maranatha Church in Palm Beach Gardens.

The Rev. Wayne Lee gave the sermon, but I don't remember anything he said or having any understanding of his message.

After the service, Bill introduced me to the assistant minister, the Rev. Lee Kizer. I later found out he was once an FBI agent who had become a Christian minister.

I told Lee of my middle-of-the-night experience.

He told me I needed to invite Jesus into my heart.

I said, "How do you do that?"

He said, "I'll say a prayer and you repeat the prayer along with me."

I did.

Nothing happened.

I went home, still feeling the same heartbreaking anguish as before.

The next day I said my first prayer - *ever!*

It was not a deep theological prayer. It was not a prayer of thanks. It was not a prayer of forgiveness for my sins. It was not a prayer for anyone else. It was a selfish prayer, a cry from the deepest recesses of my heart: *"God, I want to get back together with Vicki."*

My first prayer ever.

That was it.

Over and done with!

There were copious tears running down my cheeks.

Two minutes later the phone rang. It was Vicki. She wanted to get back together with me!

I couldn't believe it!

My prayer of just two minutes before - my first ever prayer - had been answered exactly as I had asked!

Vicki wanted to get back together with me two months after cutting off all communication.

Of course I said yes!

And we did get back together.

This phone call specifically answered my aching heart's cry two minutes after *my first-ever prayer.*

Over the next two weeks, ten things - just like that phone call - happened to me.

Ten inexplicable things.

One of those things happened while I was walking in my neighborhood reading a Bible someone had given to me. A total stranger came up to me and started talking to me about the exact verse I was reading. I stared at this person in disbelief!

Once again I was stunned.

It got to the point, over the next two weeks, where these inexplicable "coincidences" were beyond coincidence. If there were just one or two unusual, unexplainable experiences, I could easily have dismissed them as mere coincidence. But there were ten!

At that point, I recall looking up and saying something like, "God, I don't have a clue what is going on here, but I'm willing to go along."

I started attending Maranatha Church with Bill and I found the sermons inspirational.

I was given a Bible.

I began to read it.

I found it understandable. The words and passages all made sense.

And I began to learn how to pray.

Vicki and I were now back together. But it soon became apparent, to her and to me, that I had changed. Instead of us going disco dancing, I now wanted to go to church. Instead of us going to parties, I wanted to read the Bible or pray.

We stayed together for six months, but we both realized we were now on different life paths and we amicably decided to go our separate ways. We remain friends to this day.

My path had suddenly and unexpectedly taken a turn that was completely contrary to all I believed about God.

Twenty-three years earlier I had made up my mind – *there was no God.*

CHAPTER

8

St. Louis, Missouri

SHE LEFT HER HUSBAND AND THREE CHILDREN TO GO TO HOLLYWOOD TO BECOME an actress!

Doyle knew nothing of my upbringing and the dramatic night-into-day transformation about God that my life had taken. How could he possibly understand my dogged determination now to start a church?

If only I could tell him this part of my story - of the minister's wife leaving her husband and her three children to become an actress in Hollywood. And of my turnaround, twenty-three years later, to believe in God, Jesus and the Gospel.

"What?" was my response when my mother told me about the minister's wife from our church.

That experience tightly sealed both my mind and my heart to God, the Bible, any church, any religion and certainly Jesus, whoever he was.

Like most Italians, my mother had been raised Catholic. But she left the Catholic Church when she and three of her sisters moved to St. Louis from central Missouri to help out their immigrant parents.

She began attending a church that was located near Washington University, a twenty to twenty-five-minute drive from our home. My older brother conveniently caddied on Sundays at the private Normandy Golf Club up the street from our home. I was too young to do that and had to accompany my mother to church. My stepfather, who was Catholic, would drive us, drop us off and pick us up when the service was over.

The minister was an affable fellow, at times funny. And it wasn't all that painful for me to attend, though I never remember learning anything about God, the Bible or Jesus.

Was the Gospel preached? I don't recall ever hearing the word "Gospel" or the need to be "saved from our sins."

Was Jesus mentioned? Probably so, but there wasn't even one mention of the word "sin." It was just something they called "error." I never heard the terms "salvation" or "savior" or "heaven" or even "hell."

The minister's wife was a very attractive woman with an engaging personality. She and her husband had three children, all less than ten years of age. It was a fun family to be around and her birthday was the same day as mine, November 1.

For several years, it became a tradition for our families to celebrate her birthday and mine together, either at their home or at ours. This was a special occasion for me ... until she, the minister's wife, abruptly left her husband and her three children to go to Hollywood to become an actress.

It was 1962 and I was sixteen-years-old.

That did it for me!

A wall went up.

An impenetrable wall.

Forget anyone trying to talk to me about God.

Forget anyone trying to get me to go to church.

To me it was *ALL* hypocrisy!

How could she leave her husband and her children to go to Hollywood to become an actress?

It was beyond my comprehension and my mother never offered an explanation or discussion of the subject. She just kept going to this church.

But now she went alone.

I never went to that church again.

Thankfully, those teenage experiences were not the end of the story, but they blocked any belief in God for twenty-three years.

Heading to my 50th high school reunion in 2014, I was startled to find in my yearbook that there was a Bible club. It met every Wednesday morning, with more than 100 attending.

I never knew that!

But even if I had, I never would have attended. I had no interest in the Bible or in God.

Higher education, baseball and girls were my sole interests.

CHAPTER

9

Ladue, St. Louis, Missouri

DARTMOUTH ATTEMPTED TO RECRUIT ME BY INVITING ME TO AN OUTSIDE RECEPTION AT a home in Ladue with a huge rolling backyard. There must have been 250 people there.

About half were high school seniors. The other half were local alumni and Dartmouth admissions personnel.

They wanted me.

It was flattering to be sure.

Wow! An Ivy League School was recruiting me! My father had only completed high school and my mother the eighth grade.

Applicants abound every year. But historically, only one-in-ten are accepted to Dartmouth.

Perhaps my resume did it.

Senior class president of my high school.

Finished tenth out of 500 academically, with a grade point average above "A" and honors in English and mathematics.

Earned varsity athletic letters in track and cross country.

Selected to the Senior Class Saga Court (the white tie annual formal event).

I found myself in Ladue, the wealthiest town in Missouri, among many other aspiring high school seniors, the majority of whom were from St. Louis prep schools.

Their pitch was impressive.

The event was a tried-and-true effective strategy for recruiting high school students. They invited prospective students to meet local successful alumni and admissions representatives.

Dartmouth recruiters knew what they were doing by hosting their event in Ladue, the residence of many of the "Who's Who" of St. Louis business and society.

Established in 1892, the venerable St. Louis Country Club is located there. The golf course was designed by Charles B. Macdonald, who was considered the father of golf in America. The driving range, located in front of the clubhouse, also serves as a full-size polo field.

It was a not-so-subtle way of saying to the prospective high school students: "This is where you will wind up if you come to Dartmouth. Affluence, prominence and prestige await you."

Part of the recruiting pitch that evening was a profession-ally-made movie of the Dartmouth campus in Hanover, New Hampshire. It was so beautiful ... so New England.

Their appeal also focused on the opportunity for winter sports. Skiing and ice hockey were prominently featured. I had never even seen a pair of snow skis up close. It would not be until six years later that I would wind up at Vail with medical school pals, discovering the splendor of snow skiing.

Glimpses of the winter wonderland of snow didn't exactly do it for me. St. Louis winters were notorious for snow, sleet and freezing rain. Somehow, the picturesque movies of New England snow and cold didn't strike a warm cord in my mind or heart. I knew they were leaving something out.

I was pleasant to all the alumni and admissions representa-tives and expressed sincere gratitude for their interest in me, all the while feigning interest in their school.

An arctic experience wasn't for me.

My sights were already set on another "Ivy League" school.

CHAPTER

10

St. Louis, Missouri

ONE THOUSAND FIVE HUNDRED DOLLARS FOR TUITION WASN'T IN OUR BUDGET.

That was half of the annual tuition at Washington University and they had offered me a half scholarship.

High school was a stepping stone. I had done well academically, athletically and socially. My older brother had gone to the state university by virtue of a golf scholarship. Different doors were opening for me.

Highly competitive and equally highly esteemed, Washington University's doors beckoned. Just a few miles from my home, it was known locally as *"The Harvard of the Midwest."*

Consistently ranked among the top universities in the United States for Best Medical School, Best Law School, Best Business School, and noted, as well, for its School of Architecture and

Political Science Department. It drew students from every state and even some from other countries.

I was accepted.

There was just one problem.

Money.

Tuition in 1964 was $3,000 a year. That was beyond our family's means. I applied for a scholarship and was granted one, but only for fifty percent of the tuition.

The $1,500 balance would have to come from us.

We didn't have it.

That left one option: the newly-formed local branch of the University of Missouri, St. Louis (UMSL). It was established in 1963 by the Normandy School District as an affordable alternative to the private Washington University.

This UMSL satellite campus, two miles from my home, was on the original site of the 125-acre, old-line Bellerive Country Club, founded in 1897. The Georgian-style clubhouse and two classroom buildings comprised the entire school. Today, there are more than 16,000 students, with buildings covering all of the original Bellerive hilly acreage.

Though this was not Washington University, it provided another stepping stone for me.

But I never anticipated how it would unfold.

CHAPTER

11

THE NEW DEAN WASN'T PLEASED.

My recollections of my two years at the University of Missouri, St. Louis are limited to only a few activities and events.

The atmosphere of this estate-like country club setting lent itself to frivolity, highlighted by daily volleyball games just outside the clubhouse between classes. It was great fun! Because the enrollment wasn't large, about 1,000, we tended to get to know each other pretty well.

There was a small group of us that bonded, frequently partying together like students at any good state university.

One memorable event that etched its way into the St. Louis newspapers was not something this fledgling university wanted to see in the media.

During my sophomore year, our little core group decided to rent a house in west St. Louis, hire a band and have a party. A

BIG PARTY. We would charge a nominal admission and provide beer and a band. In 1965, this was going to be our equivalent of a "Blues Brothers Bash."

We rented a two-story house, got a dance band, printed flyers, told everyone we knew, bought kegs of beer and rocked. The problem was that we were a little ahead of our chronological ages.

There were at least 200 people who came, including the police.

The party was "raided," meaning that anyone under the age of twenty-one was actually taken into custody and brought to the county jail for the night. And that included me, only nineteen at the time.

We were herded into a jail cell. It was the one and only time I've been in a jail cell in my life. There were about twenty-five of us in that jail cell. It was so crowded that we couldn't sit down.

At about 3 a.m. my name was called. Someone had spilled the beans as to who the organizers were and I was one of them. All I recall is being very frightened and very forthcoming about the whole thing. We were all let go. But the raid hit the newspapers in big headlines, something like, *"UMSL Party Raided."*

The dean of this new branch of the state university was from an old Virginia family and exemplified decorum in his personal manner. He was chosen only a few months earlier. Needless to say, he wasn't impressed by our shenanigans, which ran counter to his and the entire university's objectives.

We were all put on probation. That wasn't so bad except, at the time, I was running for sophomore class president.

The dean, in a display of both his displeasure and his omnipotence, disqualified me from running.

I was so miffed by not being able to run, as I was sure I would win, that I decided I had enough of UMSL. I was going to reapply to Washington University and this time apply for a full scholarship.

Washington University not only accepted me, but gave me a full scholarship for my third and fourth years. The party thing wasn't even an issue. I guess they were more concerned with my academic life than my social life.

UMSL was in the rear-view mirror and my sights were now set on something bigger, a trait that seems to have followed me my whole life.

Or was there an unseen hand guiding me?

In retrospect, I do think the hand of God was nudging me long before I even acknowledged that God existed.

Transferring to Washington University was the beginning of my interaction with a big, big world outside of Hillsdale Drive, my home in the suburbs of St. Louis. The school was - and remains today - one of America's best in terms of academic excellence.

This private school had only 3,000 handpicked undergraduates in 1966. Each was highly competitive, highly intellectual, highly ambitious.

Everyone entered with the goal that Washington University would be a stepping stone to something greater. It was not the end. It was the means to a bigger, better and more accomplished life in the outside world afterwards.

I started Washington University as a math major.

CHAPTER

12

"YOU WILL NOT JOIN A FRATERNITY," DECLARED MY ITALIAN MOTHER.

"But I must have a social life," I argued, knowing the reputation of academically-minded Washington University and my need for a social outlet to counter the pressures of being a math major.

The Sigma Chi fraternity at Washington University was recruiting me, even though I was entering as a junior.

Though my mother had met some very conservative Sigma Chi members, she couldn't see past the potential dangers in her mind of all fraternities, which she termed "drinking crowds."

Her concern was that I would descend into a world of decadence and be thwarted from this once-in-a-lifetime educational opportunity. Perhaps my probation at UMSL from organizing that "party" had something to do with her reasoning.

She did have a point, but I wasn't to be dissuaded.

In 1966, the Sigma Chi's at WU were many of the campus leaders and, for the most part, from families of means. I'm not sure they knew that I was on probation at UMSL due to "the party," but they rushed me and I pledged as a junior.

Their declared standards resonated with me:

A Man of Good Character …
A Student of Fair Ability …
With Ambitious purposes …
A Congenial Disposition …
Possessed of Good Morals …
Having a High Sense of Honor …

The standards were written by one of the original fraternity founders, Isaac M. Jordan. They were the standards by which one would be measured for membership in Sigma Chi, which began in 1855 at Miami University in Oxford, Ohio.

Fraternity life was going to be more than just a social outlet. It was going to be an experience with a group of men who aspired to something more … from themselves and from life itself.

A pattern established itself at that time in my relationship with my *ITALIAN mother* and continued in many of my personal and professional decisions in the years to come.

I pledged Sigma Chi and just didn't tell her.

It was so much easier than to face the relentless opposition.

We had fraternity pledge meetings every Monday night for the entire first year.

I simply told my parents I was going out.

I made something up and never told them I was going to a fraternity meeting.

It worked.

She never knew.

I was loaned the money for fraternity dues from an alumni fund, which I later paid back. And this fraternity offered me the social outlet I needed while enduring the highest of academic rigors.

It was a short, but full, two years at Washington University and Sigma Chi. After being initiated into the fraternity at the end of my junior year, I was elected chapter secretary for my senior year. That meant I sat at the dais in monthly meetings, along with the president and vice president. It enabled me to be one of the last to speak on issues that came up in our chapter meetings.

Intramural sports were something that we took very seriously. My senior year, I was captain of both our intramural fast-pitch softball team and intramural ping-pong team. We won both championships that year!

The fraternity instilled in me responsible codes of conduct, as well as friendships that have endured to this day. Peter J. Stephens, an overseer of undergraduate Sigma Chi fraternities in central Florida, has been a life-long friend.

And some of us local alumni launched a Florida Gold Coast Sigma Chi Alumni Club in Palm Beach in 2014.

A bond still exists when I meet other alumni. We all had a profoundly moving initiation experience and, of course, we have our own "secret handshake."

In retrospect, I firmly believe that it was God's hand who opened the doors to the academic halls of WU, prompted me to transfer there my junior and senior years and led me to join the Sigma Chi Fraternity.

They all were stepping stones to a personal destiny that awaited fulfillment, albeit in stages, in the years to come.

The hallowed elite doors of Washington University continued to open for me, even after graduation. Although tempting, I had a different path to take, once again prompted by the unseen hand of God.

I had to distance myself from the provincial thinking of a daughter of Italian immigrants.

But it was never easy to go against *The Family*.

13

VISIT THE FAMILY. EAT RAVIOLI. PLAY "O SOLE MIO." THAT WAS THE UNSPOKEN EDICT in our half-Italian family … but wholly Italian-ruled home.

It was an unspoken rule: *"Don't venture outside the family too far."*

And then there was rule number two: *"You must be at all weekend family get-togethers. No exceptions!"*

I would always flinch at these weekend flocks of family, which always numbered between thirty and forty. One of my aunts would invariably make the request I always knew was coming: *"Dwight, play O Sole Mio."*

The request always came.

I always flinched.

And my cousins laughed, *before, after* and *during*, as I obediently played, but wished I were anyplace else. *Anyplace!*

I didn't discover there was any other food than Italian food until I pledged the fraternity at Washington University.

"You mean there is something else to eat besides pasta and there's another salad dressing besides vinegar and oil?"

The Bible later told me in Acts 17:26 that God determines the times and places people live. For me, it was being birthed into a caricature of an Italian family on my mother's side. Thankfully, I had an English father!

My Italian mother was Luigia "Louise" Argentina Ramori.

My English father was John Winthrop Stevens.

How they got together was always a mystery. But then my father was a mystery. I never knew him.

A third European country was added to the mix when I was eight-years-old by my German stepfather, George Bernard Stark.

There wasn't tension between the three countries, but each definitely had their cultural influences. Some good. Some not so good.

Let's start with the Italians, for volume always prevailed amongst the three.

Mother always emphasized how poor she was, because she was. Her education was only to the eighth grade. She repeated the eighth grade, not because she failed, but because her parents and the nuns thought she would learn even more a second year since there was no higher grade available.

Born to first-generation immigrants from Bologna, her parents came to America in 1895 seeking a better life. They didn't find it at first.

Sent to Arkansas, they became indentured servants on a cotton plantation, bound to a virtual cycle of indebtedness to the landowner. Fleeing the mosquito-infested swampy plantation after their two-year contract was up, they headed north on the Mississippi River. Anywhere would be better.

What could they do? All they knew was how to grow grapes.

Together with some French immigrants, they planted Concord grapes and thrived, eventually partnering with Welch's Grape Juice Company.

But grapes always led to another product - wine. They excelled in making their own wine, though just for home consumption.

Mother exemplified all of the typical Italian traits. She was fun-loving, exuberant, flamboyant, musical, family-oriented, argumentative, loud, stubborn, jealous and provincial.

Her best trait, though, was her cooking! She was known far and wide for her homemade beef ravioli in chicken broth. It was a delicacy.

It was her idea to name me Dwight. No doubt my being born in 1946 had something to do with that. It was the height of Dwight Eisenhower's popularity as the five-star general of the U.S. Army and Supreme Commander of the Allied Forces in

Europe in World War II. And mother liked "Ike," as Eisenhower was commonly known.

I mused that Doyle's father, also a "Dwight," must have personally known President Eisenhower. Doyle's father was a U.S. Congressman for the state of Florida when Eisenhower became President in 1953. One day I was going to ask Doyle about that.

I was with my mother to the end of her life, all ninety-nine years and nine months, mentally alert to her last quiet breath when she lay down for a nap after a lunch.

She passed on many traits to me, probably the most lingering was a love for music and the ability to play *the accordion.*

CHAPTER

14

WHAT? AN ACCORDION FOR MY BIRTHDAY GIFT? I WANTED A GUITAR!

And I'm to take lessons every week?

What?

It was 1957.

Elvis Presley's hit song, *"All Shook Up,"* was rocking the charts. The guitar was cool!

The Hula Hoop and the Slinky were popular.

Russia launched Sputnik 1.

Martin Luther King headed a nationwide resistance to racial segregation.

President Dwight D. Eisenhower ordered U.S. troops to desegregate Little Rock schools and sent federal troops to Arkansas.

And November 1, 1957 was my eleventh birthday.

What is the memorable present my mother gave me for my birthday?

An *ACCORDION!*

Yep, an accordion!

The immensely popular Lawrence Welk TV show had begun in 1955 and a featured musical instrument was the accordion, played by host Lawrence Welk and virtuoso accordionist Myron Floren.

That set the stage for my Italian mother, who envisioned her son as the second coming of Myron Floren.

I did not ask for an accordion.

I never expressed an interest in the accordion.

I did not want an accordion.

I did not like accordion music.

In fact, the next six years of weekly lessons with my teacher, Mr. Molina, was nothing short of torture. I was not allowed to go out and play ball with my neighborhood friends until *AFTER* I had practiced my 30 minutes … every day!

Italian families seem to have this insatiable need to see each other every weekend and my mother's family was no exception.

Everyone, and I mean everyone, would get together at someone's home or at a park for an all-day affair. Great home-cooked food. Our too-numerous-to-count cousins would play baseball, football or basketball, whatever sport was in season.

And I would entertain the thirty-to-forty gathered family members with *O Sole Mio, Lady of Spain, Begin The Beguine* and *Fascination,* to name a few.

My too-numerous-too-count cousins and my older brother would mercilessly tease me.

I hated it!

As much as I wanted to be the second coming of Elvis Presley with a guitar slung over my shoulder crooning *I Can't Help Falling in Love with You,* that just wasn't in the cards in this Italian family.

When I hit seventeen years old, I stood my ground and flatly declared to my mother and stepfather - no more!

No more lessons!

No more accordion!

And I stood my ground in the face of weeks of mother's incessant, but unsuccessful, attempts to persuade me otherwise.

I stopped playing … for twenty-five years … until I took my first medical mission trip to Honduras, Central America in 1988.

My mother kept my accordion in the closet of our home. She even brought it to Florida, when she and my stepfather moved here in 1977.

I thought, *let me bring the accordion to Honduras and give it away.*

And I did.

One afternoon on that Honduran mission trip, my first of many to come, I decided to lighten things up. I picked up the accordion and, somehow, a few old tunes were still in my mind. My fingers effortlessly moved up and down the keys.

They didn't ask me to stop.

They *begged me to stop.*

Nothing new.

They just sounded like all my cousins. No appreciation of *Lady of Spain.*

A few months later, I was talking by phone with our missionary in Honduras and inquired about the fate of the accordion. To my surprise, he told me that no one wanted it.

Hmmm, I thought. *"Well if no one wants it, bring it back,"* I told him.

Six months later, he did. And once again I had my accordion.

Inexplicably, I now *wanted to play it.*

I started practicing. Soon I was inviting musician friends to my home to have jam sessions. And my second accordion career was launched.

The good news is that in those tortuous early years, from ages eleven to seventeen, I learned to read and play music and to appreciate music and musicians.

Some of the most enjoyable experiences in my life have been playing the accordion, the piano and the conga drums with other musicians.

I recently learned that my mother's sister, Inez, played the accordion as did my great uncle, Victor Herbert Piazza.

I'm a third generation accordionist in my family!

Today, I play gigs with other musicians – a guitarist, a violinist, a percussionist and even another accordionist. We play before the showing of classic movies at the Paramount Church during the winter season. Among the selections: *Over The Rainbow, Besame Mucho, the theme from The Godfather, Beer Barrel Polka and Hava Nagila.*

Finally, no one tells me to stop.

They even encourage me to play more.

Thank you, mother, for giving me that accordion on my eleventh birthday.

15

HE WAS A "DANDY," SO THEY TELL ME.

I never had the privilege of knowing my dad, John "Jack" Winthrop Stevens. He was stricken with an untreatable brain infection when I was two-years-old.

Sadly, I never knew him. But I heard lots of stories about him from my mother and from his brothers and sisters.

I see some of his traits in me. He was an adventurer, a photographer and he met my mother at a dance. He even went to Florida before he met my mother, when Florida wasn't much to write home about. That was in the 1930s.

My favorite picture of him is one in which he is dressed in a jungle-style outfit, 'a la Clark Gable. Handsome guy he was. Mother said he was a "dandy."

Oh how I wish I knew him.

I was told he grew up on a plantation in Virginia, but his family lost it all in the Great Depression. His lineage is traced back to a Col. Thomas Stevens, who was born in 1633 in Deptford, England, a southeast area of London. Col. Stevens is buried in Snow, Massachusetts.

I was told my dad was a natural salesman. That's not me. But it is my brother Winthrop, who got our dad's middle name.

My dad's family was so, so different from mother's. It was fun seeing his brothers in Rolla, Missouri, but it sure wasn't like seeing mother's clan. Loud they weren't. Emotional they weren't. Argumentative they weren't. Musical they weren't. And they never cooked Italian food!

But they loved me, because I was their nephew. Even if our dad wasn't around, they made plenty of effort to see our family.

They were all entrepreneurial, ambitious, analytical, witty, wizened, proper and somewhat reserved. One uncle owned several businesses. Another uncle was a golf pro. Yep, a golf pro in the 1950s and 1960s. Not a touring pro, but a club pro in Rolla, Missouri. The golf gene must have been passed on to my brother and, eventually, to me.

Whenever we were around my dad's side of the family, practical jokes were commonplace. I even have a recollection of me playing chess with Uncle Henry when movie cameras first came out. Someone was filming us and they told me to turn and look at the camera. I obediently did. And while I turned away, Uncle Henry swiped some of my chess pieces. They *all* were like that!

Those who know me, know all too well that the prankster gene was definitely passed on to me. So watch out!

All in good fun, right?

By the way, my brother Win also has that trait. And wouldn't you know, he married someone from Lantana, Florida, Fran Sprankle. They met when he was at the University of Missouri on a golf scholarship and she was at Stephens College.

Pop was another story.

Our stepfather, George Bernard Stark, a widower, came into our lives when I was eight and Win was fourteen. The man was courageous!

What a contrast! Mom and Pop!

The Italian versus the German!

But he had a calming effect on mother. Thankfully!

And he showed us the United States.

Yes, he did.

He worked for the Terminal Railroad in St. Louis and insisted that every year we travel the U.S. by train at least once or twice. We put up no argument.

And off we went, circling the U.S. and stopping in New York, Washington, D.C., Miami, Denver, Los Angeles, Chicago, Detroit, New Orleans. We saw them all. Sleeping cars.

Dining cars. I still remember the Empire State Building, the Fontainebleau, Pike's Peak, Disneyland and Bourbon Street. It was a blast!

He had a quirk; one we never could figure out. Whenever he would cut the lawn or rake leaves, he always dressed in a long-sleeve white shirt and tie. We never questioned him about that. He was a pretty stoic German ... kind and soft-spoken and always a gentleman.

Even my dad's English family wasn't that proper.

But that was Pop. He literally took us around the U.S., while always wearing a white shirt and tie.

Life at home with mother the Italian, Pop the German, and my dad's English family was a cultural cross section, although I wasn't aware of it at the time.

But they all had one thing in common - higher education beyond college wasn't in their vocabularies.

And that's where I was headed, not exactly with their blessings.

If only I could explain all this to Doyle and tell him why it led me to start a church in Palm Beach.

CHAPTER

16

Palm Beach, Florida

"WHY DON'T YOU COME TO PALM BEACH," SAID HARRY LOY ANDERSON NONCHALANTLY, as we sat outside having breakfast at Testa's, in the balmy springtime weather.

He just asked me how my search to find a location for a church was going and I said we had not been able to find a suitable location. I told him of the many places we looked at, including a building on Clematis Street. But the realtor, who showed the building, told us the copper pipes on the air conditioning had been stolen the night before. That seemed to nix the idea right there. The location wasn't safe, a requirement that I had been advised was necessary for a church.

There was a bank building on Dixie Highway with ample parking that also could have been suitable, but the owners only would sell the property for $350,000 and did not want to rent it.

As he listened to my nomadic tales of searching without success, he presented me with an out-of-the-blue idea, "Why don't you come to Palm Beach?"

He was smiling his ever-present smile as he looked directly at me.

I mumbled, "I never thought of that."

Could he possibly be right? He was always so enthusiastic. So encouraging. So positive.

Born into a Palm Beach family of wealth and privilege, this man was one of the most charming, carefree and charismatic people I had ever met. He was Palm Beach personified.

Palm Beach?

Well, I thought, my dermatology practice for the past fifteen years was just across the north bridge, connecting Palm Beach and West Palm Beach. I had met many people from Palm Beach and had made friends with some.

"I think you should seriously think about it," Harry Loy continued.

I did.

And I began to pray about this new possibility.

What I decided to do first was to explore the idea by getting some opinions from people who lived in Palm Beach. I would send up what I called "trial balloons" to see what local Palm Beach residents thought of the idea.

Over the next two months, I asked thirty-three people from Palm Beach what they thought of the idea. Most I had met from my practice. They, amazingly, all listened to my inquiry and each seriously responded.

With absolutely no inkling of how they would respond, I found that thirty-one of the thirty-three endorsed the idea. Some very enthusiastically!

One after another after another said, "Yes!"

I was not expecting that!

But I never expected to become a doctor either.

And now medicine to ministry in Palm Beach?

Nor was I expecting what two of the thirty one who said "yes" would suggest next!

17

St. Louis, Missouri

I'M BORED! THE FIRST TIME IN MY LIFE BOREDOM HAD STRUCK.

First time!

I was twenty-years-old and bored.

It was the summer of 1967. I had just completed my third year of college, after transferring to Washington University in St. Louis the previous fall.

Through my Uncle Jewel, who was married to my mother's sister Inez, I landed a plum summer job as a temporary employee at the Monsanto Queeny Plant Chemical Company on the Mississippi River in downtown St. Louis.

It was a forty-plus hour-a-week job. Pure factory work, but good pay. Frequent night shifts. Steel-toe shoes. Helmets. Interesting work in the chemical manufacturing field.

One of my responsibilities was to trudge off to the plant's chemical lab every week with samples of the chemicals our department produced. It was there I met Charley Woodall, an African-American who was head of the lab. We somehow started talking baseball, not uncommon in St. Louis where the Cardinals permeated the culture.

He said he was captain of the Monsanto fast-pitch softball team.

I said, "Wow, I'd love to play."

Looking at me askance, he said, "If you're serious, come on out for our practice Saturday in Forest Park."

I went.

To Charley's amazement, I could hit, run fast and play center field.

They invited me to join the team and I became the starting center fielder.

Our team went to the city championship game. It was the last inning. We were tied 1-1. The opposing team had a man on second with two outs. The batter hit a hard single to me in center field. I charged, picked it up cleanly and came up firing, knowing the runner on second would be trying to score the game-winning run.

Visions of being a hero flashed through my mind as I pictured nailing the runner at the plate with a bullet-like line-drive throw. I had that kind of arm.

The ball left my hand on a perfect trajectory, just to the left of the plate, aimed to veer just enough to the right after one bounce so it would land in the catcher's mitt.

It all unfolded just as I envisioned.

Almost …

My perfect throw hit the pitcher's mound and caromed straight up in the air, never to find the catcher's mitt.

The runner easily crossed the plate.

The winning run scored. The opposing team erupted in jubilation.

We lost!

A crushing defeat.

All because of my errant throw, which was perfect in every way, except for that darn pitcher's mound! My head hung low as I ever-so-slowly headed to our dugout, where there was beer on ice awaiting. I needed *a few!*

My life should have been satisfying. I had a stimulating, good-paying, full-time summer job and played center field on a competitive baseball team.

But it wasn't enough.

The work, the play, the money, just didn't do it.

For the first time in my life I was bored.

Something stirred within me during that summer of 1967.

I had to do something else.

But what?

CHAPTER
18

Barnes Hospital, St. Louis, Missouri

"I'LL VOLUNTEER AT A HOSPITAL EMERGENCY ROOM."

One day, in that "boring" summer of 1967, a thought popped into my mind: *"I think I'll volunteer at a hospital emergency room."*

I did.

What occurred was what I now term, "my first retrospective nudge from God." At the time, I didn't realize it. It just seemed the right thing to do.

I applied to be a volunteer at the Barnes Hospital Emergency Room, the hospital associated with Washington University. I was accepted and volunteered every free hour that I could. I made my own hours and helped out wherever was needed. They were so accommodating and thankful for my assistance.

There were no doctors in our family. No one talked about medicine. No one even thought about the profession of medicine.

I had no knowledge of, or previous interest in, medicine and had *NEVER EVER* thought about medicine as a career.

But somehow, from somewhere, came this compulsion to do this volunteer work to fill my empty hours during that summer of 1967.

The experience changed my life.

Thrown into emergency room medicine was like being thrown onto a never-ending roller coaster of excitement. Patient after patient came in with every possible critical medical emergency: heart attacks, car accidents, diabetic comas, home injuries, breathing crises, stomach ailments and migraines.

Never had I seen anything so thrilling and so challenging.

The workers had a camaraderie that only those in critical-care emergency medicine can appreciate.

Right then and there, I decided that I wanted to be a doctor.

In retrospect, I firmly believe that it was God who put that idea in my mind to volunteer at an emergency room.

It didn't come from me or any of my past experiences.

It didn't come from any family member.

It didn't come from any friend.

It didn't come from any TV show or movie.

I can only describe it as coming "out of the blue," or in spiritual terms, from God Himself guiding me in His plan for my life.

My family didn't think in these terms. My circle of friends didn't think in these terms. *Nothing* in my life was geared in this direction. My studies had me leaning toward a degree in English or maybe in math.

High school and college English literature courses exposed me to the novels, short stories and poetry of Thoreau, Whitman, Dickinson, Eliot and Hemingway, all of whom expressed their thoughts on the meaning of life.

How could I apply English literature to a profession? I wanted meaning. I knew that for sure. I just didn't know what kind of career might do that for me.

And now, a whole new world opened for me … the world of medicine.

After that summer experience at Barnes Hospital, I only had one year of college remaining. To be considered for entrance to medical school, I had to complete certain pre-med courses. With the help of an understanding administrative counselor, I managed to cram all the prerequisite biology and physiology pre-med courses into my fourth year.

I soon found that other pre-med students at Washington University hoarded information, as entrance into WU's medical school was intensely competitive. Nobody shared what they knew. The thinking was, "It's you or it's me and I'm not going to let you get ahead of me."

Thankfully, grades weren't a problem for me. I got almost straight A's in every class. It was always that way for me. These pre-med courses weren't any different, just different material to absorb and memorize.

Two questions arose.

Where to go to medical school?

And … how to tell my mother that I had decided to go to medical school?

The latter loomed far, far larger than the first!

I decided to address the second question first - telling my Italian mother I wanted to go to medical school.

CHAPTER

19

"SO, WHEN WILL YOU START MAKING MONEY LIKE YOUR COUSIN WARREN?"

That was mother's response when I told her I wanted to go to medical school.

I felt crushed.

Mother ruled the roost at home. She made all the decisions in our family. She controlled what we did and didn't do.

That is ... unless she didn't know about it ... like the time I pledged the Sigma Chi fraternity at Washington University.

Her objections and reasons saddened me.

My cousin Warren, two years older than I, graduated from the University of Missouri with a math degree and began working for McDonnell Douglas as a computer programmer. I guess his achievement was considered the pinnacle to my mother and, truthfully, it was something to write home about. The scientific programming of computers was in its infancy in those days and he was really smart.

Years later, I told Warren what mother had said to me and he didn't laugh … he understood. Higher graduate school education was just unheard of to my mother and her seven brothers and sisters, including Warren's mother, Aunt Ernie, my mother's sister.

While we were sharing our common heritage, he also told me one of the funniest stories I have ever heard and can relate to as a minister.

In meeting new people, Warren said the conversation often drifts to one's occupation. When people found out he was a computer programmer, it was an absolute conversation stopper. Eyes glaze over. Silence ensues. There was never any related follow-up question, rather a pivot to something like, "Do you play golf?"

Take note, *"I'm a computer programmer"* is definitely not a cocktail party ice breaker or conversation starter!

I've experienced the same when people learn I'm a minister. Eyes glaze over. Silence ensues. There is rarely any follow-up question. It's also not all that conducive to conversation.

Back to mother's objection to my pronouncement that I wanted to go to medical school.

I was not going to be deterred.

Postgraduate studies were as foreign to my family as going to the moon, even though I had excelled in high school, was elected senior class president and had nearly a 4.0 grade average in college.

Mother's objections didn't change my ambition to become a doctor and there was nothing that could keep me in their world of family get-togethers every weekend. It was now just a question of where to apply to medical school.

There were really only two choices, both relatively local: Washington University in St. Louis and the University of Missouri in Columbia, 100 miles away from home.

But there was not even a discussion of these two options.

First, mother flatly objected even to *the idea* of medical school.

Then, after voicing her authoritarian opinion, it was settled – in *her* mind. I would find a job in St. Louis once I graduated from Washington University.

Without telling my mother, I applied to Missouri University's medical school.

I chose to apply to Missouri University and not to Washington University because I had to get away from the narrow, limited provincial thinking of my family.

Something drove me to spread my wings and I could never do that if I stayed in St. Louis near the family.

I was immediately accepted into the fall medical school class at the University of Missouri in Columbia.

The cost of going to medical school was astronomically high and essentially prohibitive to someone like me. But I applied for a medical school loan and was granted a loan for each year, enabling me to go. These loans, which reached staggering amounts, had to be paid back and they were paid back once I was in private practice.

With acceptance to medical school and a loan in hand, I once again broached the subject with mother.

She wasn't happy.

She had been outmaneuvered.

But now she could only grudgingly relent in the face of the acceptance and the loan.

My professional career in medicine was launched.

One thing remained unsettled and unanswered in my mind.

With my acceptance to Missouri University's medical school certain, the question dogged me: *"Would I have been accepted at Washington University's medical school, one of the most prestigious in the U.S. and one of the hardest to get into?"*

I had to find out.

20

THEY SENT ME A TELEGRAM.

In the short time left during the fall of 1967, I filled out the application to Washington University's medical school and surreptitiously went for interviews.

To my amazement, one week before applications closed, I received a Western Union Telegram. In those days, immediate news was conveyed by telegram, not by fax, email or even by telephone.

WESTERN UNION TELEGRAM
Jan 13, 1968, 1 p.m.

Dwight M. Stevens
7444 Hillsdale Drive STL (Via Clayton MO)

"On behalf of the Committee on Admissions I am delighted to inform you that your application for admission to our 1968 first year class has been acted upon favorably subject to the satisfactory completion of the premedical requirements and the other courses you are taking this year.

Under separate cover I am sending you a formal letter of acceptance along with pertinent documents to be completed. In accordance with the recommended acceptance procedures of the association of The American Medical Colleges I request that within two weeks from this date you file with us a statement of intent accepting our offer and including your $45.00 deposit which will be credited toward your first semester tuition payment.

Should you decline our offer your prompt reply will be appreciated. We adhere strictly to the recommended procedure that if you accept a place in our freshman class, change your mind and notify us to that effect prior to January 15, 1968, your $45.00 deposit will be refunded."

John L. Schultz
Registrar Washington University School of Medicine

In my hand I held this piece of paper telling me that I was accepted to the incoming medical school class of 1968 at one of the most prestigious medical schools in the United States and I was to notify them before the week was over.

I never met that deadline.

I didn't respond to this once-in-a-lifetime invitation.

I didn't go to Washington University's medical school.

This was one of the most difficult decisions of my young life up to that point, but I had to get away from my mother's narrow, provincial thinking.

No one disobeys Italian mothers. My mother was the queen and she issued edicts just like a tyrannical ruler. The only way around dire consequences was to simply not tell her what I was doing.

I *never ever* told my mother that I had been accepted to Washington University's medical school.

In retrospect, I believe that this decision was not just about avoiding dire consequences. Rather, it was the nudging of God directing my life along a certain path that He had determined for me. Although I was oblivious to this "guiding hand," my choices and actions were actually responses to this unseen guidance.

Although the University of Missouri's medical school didn't carry the prestige of Washington University's, it soon offered some unique opportunities for me, which included spreading my own wings away from home.

And I was about to spread my wings in some very unexpected directions.

CHAPTER

21

University of Missouri Medical School, Columbia, Missouri

THE ROLLER COASTER TREADMILL OF MEDICAL SCHOOL BEGINS.

I soon realized that medical school is like a *treadmill* that is already running. Once it begins there is no stopping, unless someone stops the machine or you fall off. But in medical school, no one stops the treadmill. You are either on for the duration or you get off.

I stayed on for the duration.

Ninety-five of the one-hundred students who started that first year with me also stayed on for the duration. Five did not. Two quit after the first year. Three during the second year. It was too demanding. They wanted their lives back.

I soon found out that you give up your life for the next four years while in medical school. And, depending upon the chosen area of medicine, your life may not be your own for the rest of your life. If I were to make it through the rigors of medical school, I soon realized that my social activities had to be minimized or even eliminated.

It was like taking college courses - times ten! Thankfully I was single. Those who were married faced an extra burden because medicine is a jealous spouse.

During the first two years, the material was not only encyclopedic, but detailed beyond description. Biochemistry, physiology, genetics, microbiology, pathology and pharmacology. It was like feeding voluminous amounts of previously unknown data into a blank computer.

And ANATOMY!

That first day in anatomy lab remains imprinted in my mind.

Lying before our team of four was the perfectly preserved body of a muscular six-foot tall man, roughly fifty-years-old. He was about two-hundred pounds when he was alive. There was no sign of trauma. No bullet wounds. Somehow his life had ended early.

But we were not there to find out why. We were there to find out about the inner construction of this physical body.

Our team meticulously uncovered his muscles, his blood vessels, his nerves, his internal organs, his joints, his brain and his spinal cord.

Wow!

There was something incredible about the intricacy of this cadaver that fascinated me. It was put together so perfectly, with attention to the tiniest detail.

I found that the hand has thirty-four different individual muscles that move the fingers and thumb, which are attached to twenty-nine different bones.

This was just the hand!

Holding a brain in my hand made me think of how an injury to one small part could affect one's thinking or ability to move normally.

Day after day was a new discovery.

I was fascinated.

At that time, I didn't believe there was a *divine hand* behind the creation of the human body. I had never read Psalm 139:13-16, which tells us that God forms our innermost being.

That would not come until *twenty-seven years later.*

Meanwhile, the first two years of medical school were pure book learning. Clinical contact with living patients would not come until the third and fourth years.

By the time I reached those clinical contact years, I would be far better prepared than those who got on the treadmill at day one and never got off.

For I was soon to slow down the treadmill.

CHAPTER

22

I SLOWED DOWN THE TREADMILL.

Some of my medical school colleagues found that being tested on each miniscule detail of the human body was grueling, unfair and unnecessary.

I found it fascinating.

So much so that when three anatomy teaching assistant positions opened up at the end of our first year, I considered applying.

Anatomy had been my favorite course the first year by far.

I liked the professor, C. Roland Leeson, a brilliant Brit with a razor-sharp wit. He gained my respect, far more than any of my first-year teachers, by his vast demonstrable knowledge of the human body and the clarity of his explanations.

He had noticed my meticulous attention to detail in the dissection of our cadaver and he would indirectly compliment my dissection work with some supremely clever remark.

He reminded me of my brother, who was a master of the same.

Dr. Leeson and I began a back-and-forth banter, which lasted the whole year. This was novel, for everyone feared him and his sharp tongue.

I thought and thought about applying for the teaching position. But if I got it, there would be a big consequence. I would have to split the second-year medical school courses over two years. Instead of completing medical school in four years, it would now take five years, but two of those years would be as an anatomy teaching assistant.

The treadmill of medical school was vividly real to me. Not that I was afraid of it or unable to cope, but here was a unique opportunity.

It was an opportunity to not only slow down that treadmill but to *teach*, something I discovered I was naturally doing with my dissection team. I had become a teacher to my other three colleagues as we cut away at our six-foot, two-hundred-pound cadaver.

And mother?

I'd just tell her, when the time came, that I was doing some extra studies or something like that.

I applied for the position.

They accepted me.

To this day, I fondly look back on those two years teaching anatomy as a great blessing for many reasons. Teaching the first-year medical students brought me into contact with new people and helped me form new friendships.

And those friendships introduced me to a part of the sports world *outside of medicine.*

CHAPTER

23

"LET'S HIT THE LINKS," SAID BILL.

My Uncle Randy was a golf pro. My brother Win received a golf scholarship to the University of Missouri after his high-school golf team won the Missouri State Golf Championship.

With this family background, surely I could play this game of golf.

Little did I know what headaches and heartaches lie ahead, buffered by the occasional, very occasional, highlight.

With an extra set of MacGregor clubs from my pal Bill Quayle, we set off to the nearby university course to escape the rigors of the around-the-clock pressure of medical school. Soon to join us were fellow med students Roger Jackson and Harvey Howitt, creating a lasting foursome.

It became apparent that all we did was replace the pressures of medical training with the pressures of competitive golf. Standing over a three-foot putt to halve a hole was actually more nerve racking than preparing a patient presentation for morning rounds.

But it was fun. Great fun.

There were nights when the darkness settled in before we were ready to head home. We pulled our cars up near the eighteenth green, turned on the headlights and putted until we gave in to the reality that we had to go home.

Those years birthed within me the love of golf, which carries on to this day. Years later, it brought me into the friendship with Bill Hobbs that led to a new life in Christ.

I've managed to play a few great courses, including Seminole, Winged Foot (East and West), Torrey Pines, Harbour Town, Bethpage (Black), Doral (Blue Monster), Quaker Ridge (Scarsdale, NY), Yale, Medalist, PGA (Champion) and Sailfish Point.

One of my indelible golf memories is punching a choked-up five iron, with a slight right-to-left draw, into a two-club wind at Seminole from 150 yards away and making the three-foot putt.

My dermatology career overlapped with golf when I wrote an article that was published in *Golf Digest* magazine in August 1980 titled, *Saving Your Skin in the Summer Sun.* My brother was advertising director for *Golf Digest* at the time, which I think might have helped get the article into the magazine. After the article was published, I was invited to an LPGA tour event in Georgia to give a talk to the lady pros on skin protection.

At one point, I was playing to an eight handicap. That led me to try competitive amateur golf. It's a quantum leap from golf with friends or even club competitions.

There is nothing like playing against serious skilled golfers. It will make all those hours of practice and visualized perfect shots disappear in an instant under the pressure!

I know. It has happened to me … more than once!

I recall playing in a county amateur tournament paired with a two handicap and a three handicap. I was an eleven handicap at that time. We started on a short 135-yard, par-3 with a small elevated green that had severe drop offs on all sides. All three of us missed the green. I was just off the green, only about ten feet from the pin. With hands shaking, I somehow managed to loft the ball using a sand wedge. It landed softly one-foot from the hole. The other guys bogeyed.

That gave me the honors to tee off on the next hole, a dogleg right, par-4 with a 150-yard carry over marsh. A 230-yard straight drive would run through the fairway. I took out my trusty three wood, planning to gently cut a fade around the dogleg.

It was one of my most memorable career shots, as I plunked it right into the marsh. I wound up with a ten on that hole. It was a very, very long day!

Thankfully, every day at golf is a new day and every round is a fresh start.

A few memorable golf quotes:

"They say golf is like life, but don't believe them. Golf is more complicated than that."

GARDNER DICKINSON

"The reason the pro tells you to keep your head down is so you can't see him laughing."

PHYLLIS DILLER

"Golf is a game which you yell 'Fore,' shoot six and write down five."

PAUL HARVEY

"Give me the fresh air, a beautiful partner and a nice round of golf and you can keep the fresh air and the round of golf."

JACK BENNY

I wondered if Doyle played golf!

Maybe that would draw him into acquiescing to my request.

And I needed to tell him that I was already teaching a Bible study in Palm Beach.

24

Palm Beach, Florida

"I THINK IT'S A GREAT IDEA AND I ALSO THINK YOU SHOULD MOVE YOUR WEEKLY BIBLE study to my home on El Dorado," was Fagi's response to my question about starting a church in Palm Beach.

Fagi Martineau had been a patient of mine in my practice for several years and I had discovered she was a devoted Christian. She didn't hide it. Although she was 80-years-old, her energy and enthusiasm was boundless and her love of Jesus was openly expressed … at least to me.

She was one of the first Palm Beachers I told about H. Loy's idea. She already knew I was teaching a Bible study at my home from our previous conversations, but I was still stunned by her answer.

"I think it's a great idea and I think you should move your weekly Bible study to my home on El Dorado," she said. "Let's see what happens when you do that."

I almost was speechless by her offer.

We had talked about being Christians during office visits, but I didn't expect she would open her home to me!

We had a group of twelve-to-fifteen people that came to my weekly Bible study in my home in North Palm Beach. I presented the idea of moving our study to Fagi's. They *all* loved the idea. All of them!

Our first study was 7 p.m. Tuesday, May 19, 1992.

Twenty people came.

We had been accustomed to beginning our studies by singing some Christian songs and we continued doing that at Fagi's. I played the accordion. Yes, my old accordion from my early years in St. Louis. It now came in handy. Portable and amenable to both upbeat joyful songs and softer reverent songs.

The group somehow thought my lone instrumental accompaniment on an accordion was just fine and they sang along with the words projected onto a portable screen that I brought along.

That first evening, I taught on the topic, "What is the Bible?"

We continued to meet weekly, each Tuesday evening, for the next six months at Fagi's home until Nov 17, when an illness in the Martineau family precluded any further weekly meetings there.

Then, unexpectedly, another door opened.

Another Palm Beach resident, Alice Howells, was attending our study. I'd known Alice for many years and was great friends with her late husband Harry. She lived on Cocoanut Row in a lovely apartment. She suggested we meet in her apartment and we did for several weeks.

Then another Palm Beach resident, Hal Scott, a past president of the Palm Beach Civic Association, offered the conference room in the Civic Association offices on 151 Royal Palm Way. We met weekly on the second floor from December 29, 1992 for almost two years.

During that time, an even bigger door opened, also unexpectedly.

CHAPTER
25

YOU SHOULD START YOUR CHURCH IN THE PARAMOUNT, JIM PARTINGTON SAID EXCITEDLY, to my utter amazement.

This distinguished British gentleman, the epitome of elegance and propriety, was not only endorsing the idea of me coming to Palm Beach to start a church, but he was also telling me where the church should be located.

I didn't know how to respond to his comment, for I had never heard of the Paramount and didn't even know where it was located. But I sure was listening, for this was a man who *knew* Palm Beach … *really knew Palm Beach*.

Jim had been a patient of mine, like Doyle, and was married to a gorgeous, elegant woman named Susan. She had been a Powers model in New York, an author of eight books, a television commentator for beauty, art and architecture, and a founding member of the Hospice Guild of Palm Beach. They had married on the island of Jamaica in 1954 and raised a family of two sons and many standard poodles in Connecticut, Martha's Vineyard and Palm Beach.

Jim and Susan were fixtures in the *best of the best* social circles of Palm Beach.

How could I not listen to him?

Here in front of me, dressed in a navy blue double-breasted blazer, pressed slacks and Gucci shoes, was one of Palm Beach's social elite. And he wholeheartedly supported my outlandish idea to launch a church on the island ... and he was telling me where to do it!

But that wasn't all.

Jim then said to me, "I'll find you a realtor. It will be easy. I'll call you tomorrow."

And with that, he was out the door.

I stared silently as he walked out. He even did that with dignity.

The next day Jim called me.

He gave me a name and a phone number, saying, "Call her. She'll handle everything for you."

Then he hung up.

I made the call, as instructed, without knowing I was talking to the current president of the Palm Beach Board of Realtors.

Jim was right.

It was easy.

We were at the Paramount looking for a vacant space within two days.

I didn't know anything about the Paramount. Nothing. Absolutely nothing.

With realtor Carol Digges guiding every step, we explored the possibility of renting a suite in this unique building on North County Road and Sunrise Avenue. And we found a vacant 1,500 square-foot suite on the first floor of the interior of the building.

We entered into a lease agreement, in which all the terms were quickly agreed upon by the owner. I then proceeded to get ready to leave for a planned medical mission trip to Honduras. If I had time, I would try to do a little homework on this interesting building.

The Paramount, at that time, was owned by the Resolution Trust Corporation (RTC), after the previous owner had defaulted on a mortgage. With the lease terms agreed upon, all that remained was to finalize the lease with their signature.

I left for Central America, fully expecting that on my return the lease would be countersigned and we would be off and running. We had agreed to all the terms. It was all settled.

So I thought.

The RTC didn't countersign the lease agreement.

Upon my return, I was informed that the RTC was selling the building and was not entertaining any new leases.

To say I was a little disappointed is an understatement. We were so close!

I learned there had been a movie theater in the Paramount and it was a Town of Palm Beach landmarked building.

It seemed like a perfect location for a church.

I continued to ask around about this building, even though our proposed lease agreement had fallen through.

Maybe I could tell Doyle about my research.

And explain to him why I was no longer practicing dermatology, even with my extensive training in the U.S. and abroad.

26

Columbia, Missouri, University of Missouri Medical School

"ELECTIVE ROTATIONS CAN BE TAKEN AT OTHER MEDICAL CENTERS IN THE UNITED States or abroad?" I asked. "And all I have to do is get there?"

Wow, that makes for some real interesting possibilities, I thought.

My third and fourth years of medical school were the clinical patient contact years and consisted of twelve two-month blocks. Eight were required and could be chosen in any sequence. Four were elective.

I was ready to start fast and did, taking the most demanding required blocks back-to-back: medicine, surgery and ob-gyn.

It was a six-month blur.

Night call was every two or three days, including weekends, and it was rare not to be called in the middle of the night. It was an exhausting, but fascinating, six months.

I thought, *let's utilize these electives right away and see what surgery is really all about in private practice.* I made an appointment with the head of the surgery department, Dr. Marion DeWeese.

Dr. DeWeese was a wonderful man, loved by everyone. To this day, there is a Marion DeWeese Excellence in General Surgery Award at the University of Missouri Medical School.

He was still wearing his green scrubs as I sat there, intimidated, looking across the desk at the chief of surgery.

I was a mere third-year medical student, who hadn't done anything on the surgical rotation except crane my neck over the surgical staff and residents to maybe get a fleeting glimpse of an operating field. My responsibilities were limited to helping the post-op patients and listening to the residents' cases on daily rounds.

A scalpel never touched my hands. I barely knew how to tie a double surgical knot and here I am asking the chief of surgery to arrange more surgical experience for me so I could actually get my hands bloody.

I didn't really know what I was asking, but thankfully he did.

He graciously listened and immediately endorsed my request, saying he'd get back to me in a few days after he made a few phone calls.

I was surprised, but oh so happy. As I left I was smiling and thinking, *boy, he took me seriously.*

Dr. DeWeese called me the next day, saying he had arranged a two-month elective in San Diego with two surgeons in private practice. I would spend one month with a general surgeon at Mercy Hospital and one month with a plastic surgeon in La Jolla.

He asked if I could do that.

I said, "Of course. That would be great. When?"

He said next month. Surgeons are like that.

Action.

Let's do it. Now!

I gulped and managed to whisper, "OK."

He gave me the general surgeon's phone number and told me to call him. I said "Thank you."

He said, "Let me know how it goes."

I said, "I will."

He hung up.

I stared at the phone.

San Diego.

I think I know where that is. California, I think.

And I went.

Those two elective externships that Dr. DeWeese arranged were to set the course of my professional life, but not in the ways I was thinking at that time.

The general surgeon was chief of surgery at Mercy Hospital and a personal friend of Dr. DeWeese. The surgeon kindly allowed me to follow him for one month in his private practice.

It was eye-opening for me to discover that general surgery was about long, bloody operations. That really shouldn't have been all that surprising because, after all, *surgery is surgery.*

Some of the procedures were five and six hours long or more. They involved removing cancerous growths from abdomens, resection of portions of the intestines or the stomach, finding gall bladders, taking out appendices and cutting through adhesions from previous surgeries of abdominal inflammations. It might seem glamorous to lay people, but the work is very hard and very tedious.

I hand it to those who are able to do this day in and day out.

It really wasn't for me.

Then there was plastic surgery.

This was another eye-opener, but not in a positive way. Maybe because it was in Southern California.

A significant number of patients didn't seem to be happy or grateful after this greatly-revered plastic surgeon performed an absolutely perfect plastic surgery procedure.

I couldn't understand it.

Patient after patient, mostly youngish women, came into his office for consultations or cosmetic procedures. There were a few scar revisions or minor trauma cases. The plastic surgeon was one of Southern California's best cosmetic surgeons.

His practice was fully booked every day and it took at least a few months to get an appointment with him. He was that good - and he was a gentleman too.

His technically-perfect operations produced flawless surgical outcomes.

The operative scars were imperceptible.

But still a number of the patients weren't happy or grateful to this exceptional plastic surgeon for his work.

It probably was typical, at least in Southern California.

Upon returning to medical school, my next scheduled rotation was psychiatry. At the end of this two-month core rotation, each of us had to write a paper on some aspect of psychiatry. Mine was titled, *Psychiatric Considerations in Plastic Surgery,* for which I won the Student Thesis Award in Psychiatry "for meritorious achievement in writing an outstanding dissertation on a psychiatric subject." The basis of my dissertation was the unhappy patients from the plastic surgeon's practice.

I did a little research on the subject in the medical library and learned that many people who seek cosmetic surgery procedures have specific expectations that their lives will be different after the procedure.

All too often these expectations are unrealistic and unmet. A cosmetic procedure, even by an exceptionally-skilled and artistic plastic surgeon, didn't always result in major life changes as the patient had hoped. Who was to blame? The skilled plastic surgeon, who had done a technically perfect procedure, was often the target. Of course, it never was the patient's fault!

Be careful, here, Dwight, I thought. *This just might guarantee a lifetime of unhappy patients and frivolous lawsuits.*

As I thought more about this, I saw the reality of what was occurring. The outward plastic surgery procedure did nothing to change the inner person. That person just had an altered exterior that maybe *looked better.*

The insides hadn't changed.

Thus, the unrealistic expectations were frequently not met, even with a better looking exterior.

This discovery lingered with me.

If this is what I was destined to face as a plastic surgeon in private practice, my future was *not* going to be in plastic surgery. At least that was settled.

So my trip to San Diego had eliminated general surgery and plastic surgery.

Back to square one.

Except for that New Year's Eve party while I was still in San Diego.

27

San Diego, California

SHE POLITELY DECLINED MY REQUEST FOR A DATE BUT KINDLY INVITED ME TO A NEW Year's Eve party that set in motion my future in medicine.

While in San Diego for the general surgery and plastic surgery externships, my responsibilities were simply to show up every day, either at a hospital or at the doctors' private offices. I also needed to find a place to live for those two months.

I arrived in the latter part of December to begin this elective schedule for the months of January and February 1972. San Diego had lots of temporary apartments available to rent and I found a large apartment complex called The Coronado. It was perfect for a short two-month lease.

The young lady who showed the apartments was very attractive and personable. Always on the lookout for a date, I asked her to go out with me. She politely declined, saying she was in a relationship. Since I was new in the area, she asked if I would like to come to a New Year's Eve party they were giving a few days later.

Of course I said yes!

This is when the gentle, guiding hand of God intervened in my life, without me even knowing it.

At this New Year's Eve party, I met Dr. Howard Milstein, a third-year dermatology resident at the University of California, San Diego School of Medicine. He unknowingly changed the course of my medical career.

Dr. Milstein and I talked about medicine and, in particular, his specialty field of dermatology.

I knew *absolutely nothing* about it.

I couldn't help but notice something very different about this fellow.

He loved what he was doing!

Almost everyone in medicine, who I had met up to that point, had both pros and cons about their chosen field of medicine. Remarkably, Dr. Milstein had *all positives* and absolutely *no negatives* about dermatology.

He was filled with enthusiasm.

He loved to go to clinics every day.

He loved going home and reading up on the skin diseases he had seen that day.

He was like a gusher at Yosemite, exuberant about what he was doing!

I was enthralled!

This was absolutely unique in my experience in medicine.

No one had this kind of attitude.

No one!

No one poured out praises and excitement and joy over their work in medicine like this third-year dermatology resident.

No one!

For more than an hour, I sat and listened to him talk about how much he enjoyed his chosen field.

What was this dermatology?

The core curriculum in medicine doesn't include dermatology. It is a medical/surgical specialty all its own.

Right then and there, I vowed to look into dermatology when I returned to school in two months.

There was a minor detour that temporarily postponed that vow.

CHAPTER
28

"TO BE OPENED AND READ TO ALL ONLY IF I DO NOT RETURN."

I came across a sealed envelope with the above handwritten message on the front.

It was my handwriting.

Vaguely remembering that I had written this, I opened the envelope to find a six-page handwritten letter dated Nov. 21, 1971, a few days before my journey to San Diego for those two surgery electives.

The first lines of the letter are a bit over-the-top dramatic:

"I write now in an effort to justify my life should my life come to an end during my trip to San Diego. These words are not written fatalistically for I have no premonition of never returning — but as a human being it must be said that

*I don't have the controlling hand as to how long I shall live
and when I shall die ...Will my car break down, will I be
robbed, will I crash – only God knows the future. I am but
a pawn in the great scheme of things. What all this means is
that if I should die at age twenty-five, I have not 'finished
my work.' No, I am not ready to die."*

I almost find it hard to believe that I wrote these words.

And to have found them forty-five years later, when God is
the center of my existence, was incredible.

Additional contents of the letter expressed a sincere appreciation of my gratitude to both my mother and stepfather for all
they had done for me.

But it is the very mention of *God* that surprised me.

I didn't believe in God in 1971, yet I mentioned God.

I never talked about God, yet I wrote as if I knew there not
only was a God, but that God controlled my destiny.

Today, without a doubt, I believe that and openly communicate that belief.

Back then, in 1971, I never discussed or mentioned God ...
AT ALL.

It had to be something or someone instilling that in me,
fourteen years before I became a genuine believer in God ...
that God existed and that He controlled my life ...

And that one day I would die …

And that God would be the one to determine when I would die.

I almost did die on the drive back from San Diego.

In Kansas.

CHAPTER
29

Salina, Kansas

I WAS PINNED UNDER THE CAR, WITH THE FULL WEIGHT OF THE 1968 PLYMOUTH Satellite on my back.

The foolishness of youth can bring unnecessary consequences. I was no exception to this axiom.

My journey *to San Diego* had been an 1,800-mile drive *by myself.*

A fraternity brother and a medical school colleague, both of whom happened to be in San Diego at the time, said they would like to accompany me on my drive *back to Missouri.*

I jumped at their offers.

Company! Good company!

"Let's drive straight through, without stopping overnight," I proposed. "We can rotate drivers."

They agreed. A great plan. We would leave early in the morning and be back in Columbia, Missouri the next day, by mid-day at the latest.

Let's go!

We set out, with me taking the first leg of driving. I drove about five hours before changing drivers. We were on our way.

I went to the back seat, stretched out, put my head on a pillow and promptly fell asleep. We rotated drivers every few hours and all was well ... until Salina, Kansas.

There the delusional belief in the invincibility of youth caught up to us. When we arrived in Kansas after midnight, my fraternity brother was driving.

I again was asleep in the back seat and felt a sensation of bouncing around uncontrollably, like rolling down a hillside. I heard no real sounds, just felt the rolling around sensation.

What came to my mind was some football advice: it's better to just relax when hit hard and let your body roll without tightening up.

I tried to do that. Let my body relax.

The next thing I knew, I couldn't move and I couldn't breathe.

I was pinned underneath the car!

My fraternity brother had fallen asleep at the wheel and the car had rolled over and over and over. The back window of this big Plymouth had popped out and I was thrown out of the back window.

The car came to rest on its wheels. I was somehow pinned underneath the car between the two rear wheels. My chin was tucked against my chest and my knees were up against my stomach with the weight of the car pressing heavily on my back.

I was conscious of being alive, though unable to move.

I felt no pain.

I just couldn't breathe.

I looked to one side and saw two sets of feet with shoes on. These two sets of feet appeared upside down to me because my head was tucked so far under me.

The next thing I knew, the car was lifted off me. I rolled over and was pulled out from under the car.

Lying on my back, I saw the stars in the sky.

There were no sounds. No people. No talking.

It was absolutely quiet.

I realized I was conscious and there had been a car accident.

I shouldn't move, I thought. Just lie there.

Still no one came. It remained totally quiet as I looked upward at the stars in the sky.

Could I move my fingers? Yes.

Could I move my feet? Yes.

Could I move my arms? Yes.

Could I move my legs? Yes.

Then I heard the sound of a siren. Help was coming. I didn't try to move anymore. I just closed my eyes and waited.

As I lay there, I felt the urgency to urinate. I took that as a good sign. As a medical student with some understanding of traumatic injuries, that meant I wasn't in shock and had no significant internal bleeding and my renal function was good. I began to feel better.

I began to shake from the cold. It was eight degrees in the middle of winter in Kansas and I was lying on frozen ground.

The ambulance arrived. There was a lot of hustling around and they put me on a stretcher. I didn't try to move until we got to the hospital in Salina.

I was examined, x-rayed and found to have two cracked ribs and swelling from some bleeding under the skin in my lower back.

I was going to be all right.

The driver had a concussion and a lacerated ear, but he, too, was going to be all right.

My medical school colleague didn't have a scratch.

Within two days, my golf buddies whisked me back to Columbia on a mattress in the back seat of a station wagon. I was hospitalized for another week and was back on the golf course in just three months, never having any residual problems from this accident.

How did I get out from under the car?

Lifting the car, a massive full-sized Plymouth, wasn't possible by two normal-sized people or even two muscular weight lifters.

What about those two sets of feet that I saw when I was pinned beneath the car? They disappeared right after the car was lifted off me. I never saw them again.

I saw no one after the car was lifted off me. And as I lay there on the freezing ground, no one spoke to me. No one checked on me. I had simply rolled over and somehow was pulled out from under the car as the unbearable weight of the Plymouth was lifted off me.

At the time, I figured it must have been two people who saw the accident. They stopped and performed a superhuman feat by lifting the car off my back.

But where did they go after that?

Why didn't they come to my aid as I lay there doing a cursory physical exam on myself?

It had to be angels. There is no other explanation.   It wasn't my time to die or be maimed.

God had protected me long before I acknowledged that He even existed.

God had a plan for me that evolved over the next decades. It was going to come to pass in spite of my foolishness. *Of that, I have no doubt!*

Once I was discharged from the medical center, the swelling in my lower back had virtually resolved on its own and I was able to walk, albeit stiffly. Just a few cracked ribs. I could manage that.

It was time to find out about that dermatology ... Dr. Milstein's dermatology.

CHAPTER
30

Columbia, Missouri

"YOU COULD GO TO NEW YORK," ANSWERED DR. ANDERSON, CHIEF OF DERMATOLOGY.

When I returned to the world of the ambulatory in Columbia, I slipped into some dermatology grand rounds, the monthly discussions of unusual cases open to anyone in the medical school.

Generally, a resident presented a case, sometimes with the patient present or sometimes by projecting slides of the dermatological condition. It was followed by discussion.

Everything was overseen by Dr. Phillip Anderson, chairman of the department of dermatology.

What I found was a man who could only be described as brilliant.

He was learned. He was articulate. He was witty. He was gracious.

As I attended these discussions, I soon discovered that he also was knowledgeable about politics, art, world affairs, music and literature. He could expound, at length, with substantive comments on almost any subject.

And most important to me, he seemed to genuinely enjoy himself in his chosen field of medicine, far more than any other professor I had met in medical school. I had to experience this new field of medicine.

I mustered up the courage to make an appointment with Dr. Anderson.

There I sat, in his tiny office, just him and me.

I expressed my interest in dermatology and told him about my encounter with Dr. Milstein in San Diego, glowing about my discovery.

I left out the car incident in Kansas.

He seemed impressed that I already had taken an elective at another medical school, since I was still only in my third year of medical school.

He began to expound on his love of dermatology. I was mesmerized.

And at the same time *totally intimidated* by this giant of an intellect.

Although I was beginning to feel sweat on my forehead, I knew I had made the right decision to talk to this man and explore his specialty.

He invited me to do an elective with him. I hadn't even thought of that. I was just fresh from California sunshine and was thinking of a repeat visit there.

Now beads of sweat were pouring down my forehead. I blurted out, "I was thinking that I might visit another medical school like I did in San Diego."

He didn't answer.

I thought I must have offended him.

He then said, "You could go to New York." He said it in such a way that it wasn't a direct answer as much as he was thinking out loud.

Without hesitation, I said, "Well, I've been to New York. Is there somewhere else could I go?"

I visited New York on several occasions and didn't see myself blending in as a Midwesterner.

Without blinking he quickly retorted, "You should go to New York."

This time he wasn't thinking out loud. It was a definitive answer.

What was he thinking?

Did he know something I didn't know?

Of course he knew everything. He was, without a doubt, the most intelligent man I had encountered in my life at this point.

He surpassed any professor I had met at Washington University.

New York?

Anyplace but New York!

Although I didn't know it at the time, he was laying the foundation and giving me the key to my entire professional medical future.

I had no idea that was happening.

I went to New York.

CHAPTER
31

"DOES HARVARD HAVE A DERMATOLOGY PROGRAM?" I NAIVELY ASKED DR. ANDERSON.

He must have thought I was from Missouri. I was!

Of course Harvard had a dermatology program! It was at Massachusetts General Hospital, headed by Dr. Thomas B. Fitzpatrick, author of the most authoritative reference book on dermatology. He was considered a "superstar" in dermatology. Some called him the "father of modern academic dermatology." He held an M.D. with a Ph.D. in pathology.

My simplistic thinking was, *"Well, if I'm going to New York, Harvard is kind of in the neighborhood. I'd like to see that too, 'cuz I'm just not thrilled about New York."*

Dr. A, as Dr. Anderson was called, smiled at me and took my naïve request seriously. He arranged an elective externship for me in dermatology at New York University Skin & Cancer Unit as well as at Massachusetts General in Boston.

Talk about life-changing.

I was about to embark on the path that would determine my future medical career.

I packed up a few things, undaunted by the futile excursion that ended in Kansas. I set out, by myself, driving to New York in yet another Plymouth, which was kindly provided by my forgiving stepfather. The first one, also his, remained in a scrap heap in Kansas.

This time I stopped and rested along the way.

When I got to New York City, I found the biggest issue wasn't finding a place to stay. It was where to park my car. Thankfully, NYU had a parking lot for the medical staff.

Day one at NYU Skin & Cancer Unit brought me face-to-face with Dr. Stu Tobin, a recent University of Missouri Medical School graduate. We didn't know each other that well, but we recognized each other. He immediately took me under his wing. It was like I had a big brother watching over me.

I asked Stu where I might stay for the month. He said that was easy. "Stay in the call room at Bellevue Hospital," he said. "Nobody stays there when they are on call."

I did. That was settled.

And my month at NYU began.

There were seventeen full-time physicians on the dermatology staff, at least forty-five part-time physicians, twenty-seven residents and seventy in-patient hospital beds designated just for dermatology at NYU, Bellevue and the Veterans Administration Hospital. The buildings were next to one another on First Avenue.

It was big time dermatology!

Dr. Leonard Harber, one of the seventeen full-time staffers, oversaw my month-long elective. I carefully logged every dermatological condition that I saw during the day clinics and turned that extensive log in to Dr. Harber at the end of each day. This wasn't required and he was amazed at the intensity of my interest.

The seventy in-patient dermatology beds, unheard of anywhere else, were filled with rare and/or hard-to-treat dermatological cases. There were patients with pemphigus vulgaris, bullous pemphigoid, scleroderma, dermatomyositis, leprosy, erythrodermas and deeply invasive recurrent basal cell carcinomas. These rare conditions were the norm, not the exception at this program.

We were often called to see hospital consultations for drug reactions and systemic infections.

The skin cancer division, headed by Dr. Al Kopf, treated case after case of malignant melanomas, basal cell carcinomas, squamous cell carcinomas and Bowen's disease.

At that time, dermatological surgery was just beginning to take hold. There was a new technique of skin cancer microsurgery called Mohs surgery. It had just begun with Dr. Perry Robins at the helm.

After the one-month elective at NYU, I was flying high. New York City was a never-ending place of discovery, especially to a Midwesterner.

My one month at NYU was a thousand times better than I expected. Dr. Anderson was right when he said, "Go to New York." I later discovered that this program was the world's best and largest, but I didn't know it at the time.

It was time to move on to Massachusetts's General. After finding an apartment in Brookline, I embarked on the second leg of my dermatology adventure. I didn't tell anyone at Mass General that I had spent the previous month at NYU.

It was a good program, but smaller. Much smaller. It had about twelve residents, whereas NYU had twenty-seven.

There were clinics, but no surgery. There were conferences, but only the full-time staff of seven or eight attended. There were few outside practicing physicians in attendance.

In the daily clinics, I stood out. They couldn't understand why I knew so much about dermatology. Dr. Fitzpatrick nick-named me "The Missouri Flash." Here was the author of the biggest, most exhaustive dermatological text to date and he was impressed by me.

His book impressed me. He didn't.

I thought he was haughty.

He sat in his designated chair at conferences, always dressed in a three-piece suit, carrying a loupe, watches, a wallet and a book of aphorisms. Everything was attached by chains across his chest as he puffed on a tobacco-less pipe.

Although it was an enchanting city, Boston didn't impress me as much as New York City.

I drove back to Missouri, again stopping to rest, knowing that I was sold on dermatology.

I had been to the mountain and it was the mountain I wanted to climb.

I met with Dr. Anderson and told him of my experiences. He already knew, since dermatology was a pretty small world within itself.

He told me that both programs would welcome me if I wanted to go to either place for my dermatological residency.

I was amazed.

NYU even made a formal offer of a three-year residency to begin after I completed a one-year internship.

And this was when I was still just a third-year medical student!

Of course I accepted NYU's offer, even though I had another full year of medical school plus one year of internship some-where to complete.

And I had two more electives in that last year of medical school.

With a guaranteed dermatology residency in my pocket, maybe Dr. Anderson would have some thoughts about those elective months?

Of course he did, expanding my world even further.

CHAPTER

32

London, England

"WHAT SHOULD I DO NOW?" I ASKED DR. ANDERSON.

He was right about me going to New York.

He had made it possible for me to be offered a three-year dermatology residency at NYU Skin & Cancer Unit as a third-year medical student.

What else did this wizard have up his sleeve?

Once again, I gathered up the courage to make another request of the man who had orchestrated my future in medicine.

Once again, I sat in his office with another question.

This time I wasn't sweating.

But I was still in awe of his intellect, his knowledge and his influence that far exceeded mine.

I said, "Dr. Anderson, as you know I have been accepted for a residency in dermatology at NYU thanks to you."

He nodded.

No comment was necessary. He knew that it was all his doing.

"I have some free elective time left this last year. Perhaps I could do some more dermatology somewhere?"

He paused. His eyes darted here and there. With a wry smile he asked me, "Are you willing to go London?" He was staring at me without blinking.

I gulped.

Not knowing what to say, I stole a glance around his office seeing books about opera and world leaders.

I was silent.

He was silent.

We continued looking each other, neither one blinking.

Finally, I muttered, "London?" My eyebrows went up as I spoke.

Without a pause he said, "That would be a good place for you to see and experience a bigger picture of the world of dermatology."

"Uh, how could that be possible?" I asked, barely above a whisper.

"I'll arrange it, if you can go."

Can I go? I thought. *Of course I can go.*

Wow!

What is he thinking now?

"You can arrange that?" I asked.

"Sure. Easy. Great place for you. You already have a residency at NYU. Why not see some more dermatology from another expert in our field?"

"Another expert?" I quizzically asked.

"Charles Calnan. He's one of the best in our field," he said.

"And he's in London?" I asked.

He answered, "At St. John's Institute. You'll love it. Right in the heart of London. Think about it."

I was speechless. I was anticipating another stateside trip to another medical school, but not a transatlantic one.

Dr. Anderson had proven he knew what he was talking about, sending me to NYU and Mass General. This was no time to question him. He had gotten me a residency in dermatology as a third-year medical student. This man was not to be doubted in his knowledge or influence.

"OK. Go ahead and arrange it," I said.

"Good. I'll be in touch. Have to go now. Have some residents waiting for me."

And he was gone in a flash.

I sat there not able to move.

What was he up to this time? London?

How could I ever tell mother this one?

New York was more than she could handle. Now London?

To London I went. To St. John's Institute for Diseases of the Skin in Leicester Square, right in the heart of London.

Eye-opening is a whopping understatement.

This was now England.

Europe.

My first trip outside the continental United States, except for a brief jaunt once to Paradise Island in the Bahamas.

The chairman of dermatology at St. John's was world-renowned dermatologist, Dr. Charles Calnan, a professional colleague of Dr. Anderson's. But then again, "Dr. A." seemed to know everybody in dermatology.

Dr. Calnan was a true English gentleman, who personally welcomed me and mentored me for my one-month elective. He had worked in the U.S. with Dr. Albert Kligman and Dr. Walter Shelly in Philadelphia and was an expert in contact dermatitis. He readily shared his expansive knowledge.

Why else did Dr. A. recommend St. John's, I wondered.

I discovered that St. John's was Britain's leading skin hospital, founded in 1863 by a surgeon, John Laws Milton, whose career was cut short by hand eczema. The condition was severe enough to prevent him from operating, apparently causing him to establish a branch of medicine in London just for skin diseases.

Wow!

London!

"How ya gonna keep 'em down on the farm after they've seen Paree'?" went the song by Nora Bayes in 1919.

That sure applied to me, going from the suburbs of St. Louis to the steps of Buckingham Palace.

I learned how to pronounce "Leicester" Square, which took a little doing since there are only two syllables in "Leicester," not three. All around were the vestiges and customs of the British Empire, including the ubiquitous theaters, pubs, two-tiered buses and Indian restaurants.

And everyone sounded so British! My American "accent" definitely stood out!

I found a B&B to stay in near Hampstead Heath, a large park just a few miles from central London. Breakfast was markedly dissimilar to my usual eggs, bacon, toast, waffles, pancakes, oatmeal and/or cereal.

There was toast with jam and tea.

And more toast with jam and tea.

More often than not, I left the friendly breakfast table hungry, yearning for a waffle.

I decided to make this once-in-a-lifetime experience a two-part trip, just like going to New York and throwing in a trip to Boston.

Dr. A. consented to my two-part plan. In fact, he loved my idea. It was going to be one month at St. John's and one month of hitchhiking through France and Spain. As I explained my proposed itinerary, there was something in his expression that seemed to reflect a wish that he could still do the same.

After my month in London, in spite of speaking no French and only faint remembrances of my four years of high-school Spanish, I crossed the English Channel and proceeded to thumb my way through France and Spain. I ended up in Torremolinos on the Costa Del Sol. That last stop was two memorable weeks of meeting and having beers with people from *all over* the world.

Then home beckoned, with one more elective externship in cardiology at M.D. Anderson in Houston. I learned about EKGs, but I could never seem to hear the heart murmurs that everyone else claimed they heard.

That cemented my calling to dermatology.

If I could *see* a problem, I was far more likely to make a diagnosis.

It was now time to graduate medical school, match for a one-year internship and begin my guaranteed three-year residency in dermatology at NYU.

But I didn't match.

33

Columbia, Missouri

"SO I DIDN'T MATCH. NO BIG DEAL. I HAD A DERM RESIDENCY ALREADY LOCKED UP."

Internships, the grueling one-year of medicine that everyone dreads, are determined by an ordeal called "matching." It's the link between the end of medical school and the start of an internship. One could even say it was a time when we "sweated bullets." It was that stressful.

The way it worked was simple: one applied for internships at different medical schools and the school that accepted you into their program was termed a "match."

I already had a three-year dermatology residency granted to me *AFTER* a one-year internship. So an internship was just a "passing through period" as far as I was concerned.

Most medical students were still in the searching stage of their medical careers. Mine was already determined. It was something my fellow medical students couldn't believe and openly envied.

Most apply at many different places for internships, sometimes five or more. It is that uncertain. I applied to two programs, arrogantly requesting that a component of my internship include dermatology because I already had a residency offered to me.

Neither school was interested. Both said no.

I didn't match.

Only two out of my one hundred classmates didn't match.

It was embarrassing, except I had my three-year residency in my back pocket.

And then God opened a door, when there literally wasn't a door.

I went to Dr. Anderson and, feeling humiliated, told him I didn't match.

He wasn't concerned.

He had an idea.

NYU had just begun a split internship, six months of medicine and six months of dermatology. It had never been done before. Dr. Anderson told me to apply.

I was wide-eyed in wonder.

It took me about two seconds to agree.

I applied.

I was accepted.

NYU took me into that new pilot program, with a guaranteed three-year residency afterwards.

To come from not matching to getting the absolute *best possible* internship left my medical school friends in shock. They couldn't believe it.

I could hardly believe it. A six-month medical internship, then three-and-a-half years of dermatology!

Even mother, after she got used to the idea of me going further away from home, marveled at my stroke - of what she termed - "luck."

In retrospect, it had to be the hand of God, matching me to a program that never existed before, long before I even believed that He existed.

Off to New York I went for the next four years, with Dr. Anderson's blessing.

CHAPTER
34

New York, New York

THE NYU DERMATOLOGY PROGRAM ACCEPTED NINE RESIDENTS EACH YEAR, WITH ONE or two of the nine usually from a foreign country.

Missouri was like a foreign country to New Yorkers, so I think I qualified.

On the first day, the chairman of the department, Dr. Rudolf Baer, welcomed us. Born in Austria, Dr. Baer was the epitome of a European aristocrat. His noble bearing emanated from everything he said or did. I was fascinated.

His patients were referred from all over the world. Yes, all over the world people knew of Dr. Rudolf Baer.

He invited us to his Park Avenue apartment for dinner. This was a *whole new world to me.* Dr. Anderson hadn't prepped me for this ascent into aristocracy.

His right-hand man was Dr. Al Kopf, probably the world's most knowledgeable dermatologist on skin cancers, in particularly melanomas. He was the definition of the word "meticulous" with his approach to diagnosis and treatment.

And then there was Bernie.

A. Bernard Ackerman.

Or "A.B.A.," as he sometimes was known in inner circles. His initials were sufficient for identification.

Bernie was a dermatopathologist, par excellence. His realm was examining skin biopsies microscopically. That's where diagnoses are made and treatments determined.

When Bernie spoke, everyone listened. Even Dr. Baer and Dr. Kopf didn't tower over everyone like A. Bernard Ackerman.

Bernie stood six-feet five-inches tall, with an academic pedigree from Phillips Academy in Andover, Mass. and degrees in philosophy and theology from Princeton, Columbia, Harvard and the University of Pennsylvania.

We cowered before him, all the while mesmerized by him. His physical stature gave him the appearance of a professional football tight end. This was not a man to take lightly. He could and would verbally swat away those whom he deemed beneath him.

Exclusive knowledge was his advantage and intimidation was his game.

He had an unequalled command of the English language, interspersing words we might have heard once in our lifetimes but had *never* used in a sentence.

He *always* had the last word! And justifiably so.

Quickly I assessed this new realm.

It was a virtual Who's Who and What's What of dermatology, every day in every way.

I was one of twenty-seven residents who would be assigned at various times to New York University Skin & Cancer Unit, the V.A. Hospital and Bellevue Hospital.

Dr. Michael Reed and I began our residencies together … our first assignment was at Bellevue! That planted a seed for a life-long friendship that has continued to this day, albeit Michael stayed in Manhattan and I headed south.

When we entered the elevator of the "Old Bellevue," a grisly elevator operator would ask, "What floor?" He would proceed to close, by hand, the metal collapsible door and we would ascend. It was pure antiquity, until the "New Bellevue" was built two years later.

I'll never forget the patient who had an around-the-clock armed guard in his room because he had allegedly murdered someone.

And then there was the fellow from whom we couldn't draw blood. All his veins had been used up from injecting drugs. He asked us one day if perhaps he could draw his own blood for us.

We agreed. He asked for a belt and a syringe. I gave him my belt. He wrapped the belt around his right bicep and took the other end tightly in his teeth.

With his left hand shaking, he stuck the syringe into an area near his elbow and proceeded to aspirate a syringe full of blood.

He knew where his remaining veins were.

We were speechless at his performance.

Wow!

My first junkie.

Then there were afternoon clinics. Pimps, prostitutes and crossdressers, all dressed to the hilt, came into these clinics. For a kid from Missouri, this was a "welcome to the real world" experience that one *never forgets.*

And then there was the emergency room visit one night to see a patient with a severe skin reaction from a medication. In stumbled a fellow with a meat cleaver deeply imbedded in his back. It was planted there by his girlfriend.

Ah, Bellevue!

But back to Drs. Baer, Kopf and Ackerman.

They were the backbone of the residency program.

Near the end of my first-year residency, I concocted a plan. Could I gain more access to these three men?

I made appointments with each of them: Bernie, Dr. Kopf and Dr. Baer. "Can I work with you?" I asked each of them.

To my amazement, they each said, "Yes."

Bernie and Dr. Kopf had research projects. I became their personal assistant, with direct access to these towering intellects almost every day for the next two years.

Dr. Baer allowed me, for a time, to be the first contact person with his private patients. I would ask them why they were seeing Dr. Baer and do a cursory exam. Then Dr. Baer would enter the room, formally shake the patient's hand, sit down in a chair, cross his legs, take off his glasses and chew on one arm of his glasses as if it were a pipe.

He listened to my very brief presentation. He wanted brief! He got brief!

If I or the patient went on too long, he would begin to bounce his crossed leg or tap his foot. We all quickly learned this wasn't a good sign, neither for the dermatology resident nor the patient. One didn't waste his time.

I wrote papers for Bernie. He was like a human dictating machine, with brilliant soliloquys interspersed among the medical facts.

I also wrote papers for Dr. Kopf and gave presentations of his research findings.

The experience was grand in the extreme.

Living in Manhattan was grand in the extreme.

Dr. Anderson had sent me into the heart of the world of dermatology.

A kid from Missouri.

And through this new world I met another lifelong friend, Dr. Arthur Lebowitz, an internist and infectious disease specialist at NYU. Medicine started our friendship; humor and golf continued it.

Coincidentally, while I was at NYU, my brother was working in New York City at that time as advertising director for Golf Digest. He commuted from Darien, an upscale Connecticut suburb. He would invite me to spend weekends with his family, as a brief respite from the rigors of the residency.

There was one weekend I'll never forget.

CHAPTER

35

Mamaroneck, New York

I BROUGHT VENERABLE WINGED FOOT GOLF COURSE TO ITS KNEES WITH THAT SHOT.

Well, maybe that's an exaggeration. But it sure seemed like the greatest golfing triumph of my less-than-stellar golf career.

New York City was my abode for four years from 1973 through 1977 and the "concrete jungle" was my lair. Venturing out was limited due to the rigors of internship and residency.

There were a few jaunts to Long Island, Coney Island, New Jersey and once to Boston and Maine. But for the most part, journeys out of the confines of Manhattan were out of the question.

Except to visit my brother.

My older brother, Win, worked in New York City. It was the first time we ever had been in the same locale for more than a few days, since growing up in St. Louis. Our lives were on markedly different paths. Mine was medicine. His was the corporate world of advertising and magazine publishing.

Win commuted into the city and settled into his office as advertising director with Reader's Digest in the Pan Am Building on Park Avenue. This eventually led to a position as advertising director at Golf Digest, with offices in Manhattan and Stamford, Conn.

Ascending quickly up the corporate ladder and enmeshed in the corporate world of golf, he knew that a helpful "necessity" for his work was a prestigious golf club membership to schmooze with clients.

He insightfully set his eyes upon the *Winged Foot Golf Club* in Mamaroneck, New York, a mere twenty-three-minute drive from Darien.

A perfect choice!

Winged Foot rose above most clubs with two treacherous eighteen-hole layouts, lightning fast contoured greens and a sterling history of both professional and amateur championships.

Founded by a consortium consisting mainly of members of the New York Athletic Club, Winged Foot gives one a sense of golf lore even on the driving range. Pros are dressed in slacks, long-sleeve dress shirts and ties, even in the sweltering summer heat and humidity.

On occasion, Win would invite me to spend a weekend with his family in Darien, which always included a Saturday round of golf at Winged Foot.

These invitations were a breath of fresh air for me. Heading out to wooded areas seemed a world away from "The City."

With barely a repeatable golf swing, I showed my rustiness and was glad to drown the despair of the embarrassing day with a beer or two in the clubhouse after the round.

Until that one day.

The match was best ball with my brother and two of his advertising friends.

The banter was relentless.

The needling began before the first tee and never abated.

I was paired with a ruddy-faced fellow in his forties, whose complexion broadcast the effects of far too many three-martini lunches.

My brother and another fellow were the competition. Win's partner was not only a bit disheveled, but his occasional guttural, monosyllabic utterances gave clues that he seemed to have been up all night.

The match miraculously was tied going to the tough par four number eighteen on the west course, just below the clubhouse terrace. It was playing 430 yards from the black tees. Barely a breeze from right to left. There wasn't a gallery. Who would be interested in watching us anyway?

Well, they should have been.

After a good drive and a very slightly pulled three-iron, I was lying two, buried in four inches of deep grass, just off the green.

The shot would have to be perfect or the ball would start rolling and rolling down the sloped green, requiring at least a twenty-foot come-back putt.

I loved these delicate around-the-green manufactured shots, 'a la Phil Mickelson, and often had friendly competitions with friends at practice greens. We challenged each other with imagined "up and downs."

I even told the caddy to pull the pin and laughter exploded from our opponents.

My partner was mute, stunned into silence by such a ridiculous request.

Taking a sand wedge with the blade wide open, I made a swooshing swipe through the deep grass, popping the ball up three feet in the air, along with a cascading shower of blades of grass that fluttered downward like falling snow.

The ball landed three feet short of the cup.

It landed perfectly.

I held my breath, envisioning it all.

The ball did a tiny hop, then began to slowly ... very slowly ... roll and roll. Much to the surprise and chagrin of my brother and his monosyllabic partner, it disappeared into the cup.

Holed out from an impossible lie!

A birdie!

Just as I visualized it!

We had won the match!!

I let out a primal scream when the ball dropped into the hole. It no doubt initiated a complaint letter from the golf etiquette committee for my unacceptable public outburst.

That wasn't all.

Earlier, I nailed an ever-so-slightly, right-to-left four-iron to fifteen feet from the pin on the par three, 190-yard signature hole ten. It was the hole that Ben Hogan described as "like trying to hit it in someone's bedroom," referencing the small house behind the green. I didn't make the winding side hill putt, but managed to stop it eighteen inches below the hole and easily dropped the par putt.

We won that hole too!

CHAPTER
36

Greenwich Village, New York City

"LET'S TAKE A JAZZ DANCE CLASS IN GREENWICH VILLAGE," WAS THE PLEA FROM MY girlfriend. It was the last year of my residency at NYU.

Dianne was athletic and aerobic and she thought it might be something fun we could do together.

Her request elicited a non-disguised, dismayed and contorted facial expression, one I didn't even try to hide.

I'd never had such a request.

Needless to say, I dismissed her suggestion.

A few weeks later, she nonchalantly brought it up again.

The second time around I wasn't so dismissive, but still didn't respond in the affirmative.

Then she changed her tactics. Dianne softly purred about how much fun it would be to dance together in addition to our occasional visits to Manhattan night clubs, which we loved.

Her persistence paid off. I was out of protests.

I agreed.

One Saturday morning, we went to an aerobics class in the Village, where simple jazz routines were taught to adults. Everyone seemed to be a beginner, so I didn't feel out of place. While always somewhat of an athlete, learning specific dance steps definitely was new to me, but I haltingly admitted that I did find it kind of fun.

We kept going.

New York City can do that to people. Adventures wait around every corner in the Big Apple.

The music awakened within me some semblance of athleticism coupled with rhythmic motion. I liked it and it became a regular thing we did together.

Years later, around 2003, along came ballroom dancing, which started from watching a movie titled "Assassination Tango" starring Robert Duvall. In the film he goes to Argentina and dances tango with a professional tango dancer.

I sat there watching the beauty of their dancing together and recalled the great fun it was to dance with Vicki and Dianne. In fact, it was the most fun I'd ever had.

The wheels began to turn.

Could I dance again?

I didn't have a partner.

Months before, a friend of mine, Ken King, mentioned that he enjoyed ballroom dancing. At the time, I responded with silence and changed the subject. But I recalled his words and his enthusiasm. I called him.

He gave me the name of a ballroom dance teacher, Denise Lazo. I started taking ballroom lessons at a dance studio in Delray Beach with Denise. The dances included waltz, rumba, cha cha, fox trot and tango.

I liked it.

Denise suggested that she and I participate in monthly showcases at the studio, which entailed preparing a choreographed dance routine.

I said OK, having no clue as to what lies ahead.

I didn't know that she had won at the highest levels of competitive ballroom dancing in the United States.

She was a pro.

Our choreographed routine was memorable. I have never been more petrified than when the music started and we walked out onto the dance floor with the spotlight on us. I totally forgot everything we had rehearsed. The man usually leads in ballroom. Not this time. Denise led me through the whole routine. That's the only way we made it through.

But then she was a pro!

With her kind encouragement, this led to more than a dozen competitive events, complete with tuxedos and numbers on my back. Amazingly, we frequently won these competitions! We even performed several ballroom routines before classic films at the Paramount, one of those to *You Were Never Lovelier.* It was a takeoff of a routine Fred Astaire and Rita Hayworth did in the film.

People still remember those dances and ask me to perform again. One day I hope to.

I believe there are "dancers" and there are people who dance.

For the first category, something inside the "dancer" connects to the music and the dance just comes naturally, though the steps must be learned.

Today, the Latin dances of salsa, cha-cha, rumba, bachata and hustle have presented a whole new genre of music and dance steps for me.

I was told by a fantastic salsa dancer, Latin by heritage, that all Latin people began listening to salsa music in the womb. It is a little more challenging for someone who is half-Italian and half-English, but I must admit it is fun trying, as long as my creaky joints permit.

37

West Palm Beach, Florida

"COME JOIN MY DERMATOLOGY PRACTICE IN FLORIDA," JOHN SAID TO ME ON THE phone.

"Thanks, but I really don't think so," was my reflex response. "I'm just starting my second-year residency and am two years away from being able to start private practice."

He was asking me far too early.

"When you have vacation time, think about coming for a visit," he answered.

"OK, I'll do that. But I don't think Florida is for me," continuing to express my reluctance.

"Sure, I understand," he said. "But if you'd like to relax and escape from the pace of New York City, come and visit Jan and me here in West Palm Beach," he persisted.

"OK. I'll keep that in mind," I said not wanting to be rude. Florida?

Practice dermatology and live in Florida?

Never!

I'd been to Florida several times with my parents. My thoughts reverted to my memories of those vacations to Miami Beach.

Collins Avenue.

The Fontainebleau.

The Diplomat.

Sunny and hot.

Too many high rises.

Old people.

I had been to Florida twice on spring break with my Sigma Chi fraternity brothers. Now that was different. It was fun, fun, fun. Five of us piled into Steve Brint's burgundy convertible and shot out of St. Louis two years in a row to do our '60s version of the boogaloo in Fort Lauderdale. It was a blast!

But live there?

Too much partying … all the time.

Nah, I didn't think Florida was for me.

About a month later, John called again, asking if I was coming down. It was pretty dreary, with blizzard conditions in New York. It wasn't even possible to go to my place of refuge, Central Park. New York comes to a stop when it snows. It is a welcome, but short-lived, respite from the frantic pace.

He was persistent.

A visit to Florida?

"I'll get back to you," I said.

As I looked out the window at the snow, I began to seriously think about his invitation.

Three months later I was in Florida, visiting Dr. John Kinney, who had been a dermatology resident at NYU with me and had finished his residency two years ahead of me.

We were good friends. John was one of the hardest working, brightest and most committed physicians I ever met. He was a serious physician and he also was athletic. We used to work out together at the venerable McBurney YMCA on West 14th Street. After completing his residency at NYU in 1975, he joined the prestigious Palm Beach Medical Group.

John walked into a full practice on day one and immediately needed an assistant.

He started recruiting me to join him when I had just started my second year of residency. I hadn't given one thought to where I might eventually start a private practice, after completing my three-year residency.

With the help of Drs. Baer, Kopf and Ackerman, I joined the Palm Beach Medical Group. New doctors joining the medical group had to be pre-approved by the entire group, which at that time numbered around twenty-five doctors. Drs. Baer, Kopf and

Ackerman each provided glowing written recommendations, which paved the way.

I joined the medical group in September 1977, beginning my private practice of dermatology.

Thirteen years of preparation was now finally complete.

I was about to realize my life's goal after four years of undergraduate study at University of Missouri St. Louis and Washington University, five years at Missouri University Medical School and four years as an intern and resident at New York University.

Many people from Palm Beach came to the medical group. I didn't know it at the time, but Doyle Roger's office was in the Royal Poinciana Plaza, just across the bridge from my office.

Doyle would become a patient of mine.

Also, just across the bridge was the Paramount.

CHAPTER
38

Palm Beach, Florida

"THE PARAMOUNT IS A LANDMARKED BUILDING," SAID THE WOMAN AT THE HISTORICAL Society.

"What does that mean?" I naively asked.

"It's a National Historic Landmark, designated so by the Library of Congress," she explained, "and it is a Palm Beach town landmark. You are welcome to take a look at our file."

I did. It was two inches thick.

It was like opening a Pandora's Box!

I didn't know anything about the Paramount.

I didn't know that the original owners of the Paramount were E. F. Hutton, Anthony J. Drexel Biddle Jr. and J. Leonard Replogle.

I didn't know Hutton had a brokerage office in the front of the building when it opened on January 9, 1927 with the film *Beau Geste* starring Ronald Colman. The movie opened to a full

147

house comprised of the top echelon of Palm Beach's elite society. A twelve-piece live orchestra and Wurlitzer organ accompanied the silent film.

I didn't know that *Photoplay Magazine* ran a story in 1927 on the Paramount titled, "The Millionaire's Movie Theatre," noting that twenty-six bodyguards were in the audience for that first movie because the ladies in attendance were so bejeweled.

I didn't know the twenty-six balcony boxes were dubbed the "Diamond Horseshoe" by the *New York Times*. Those balcony boxes sold for $1,000 each for the fourteen-week season, which ran from the end of December to the beginning of April. At the end of "the season," the theater closed until the next December.

I didn't know that the Paramount was designed by noted Austrian architect, Joseph Urban, a set designer for the Metropolitan Opera as well as the Ziegfeld Follies.

I didn't know that he had already made his unique mark in Palm Beach, designing the Bath & Tennis Club and completing Mar-A-Lago for Marjorie Merriweather Post.

I also didn't know that Urban designed the Paramount as a dual-usage complex, with retail shops, a restaurant and offices facing North County Road and Sunrise Avenue. It also had an inner courtyard, which led to a movie theater in the interior.

I didn't know that the Kiwanis Club held annual benefits for underprivileged children each year from 1927 to 1959 and their board included Arthur Hammerstein, Flo Ziegfeld, Billie Burke,

Irving Berlin and George Gershwin. They brought in the biggest names of stage, screen, radio and television.

I didn't know that among those who appeared at the Paramount for charitable events and/or special performances through the years included Eddie Cantor, George Jessel, Al Jolson, Danny Kaye, Sophie Tucker, Will Rogers, Sergei Rachmaninoff, Bob Hope, Robert Merrill, Ed Sullivan, Duke Ellington, Eugene Ormandy, Anna Moffo, Helen Hayes, Van Cliburn, Beatrice Lilly, Jerome Kern, Maurice Chevalier, George Hamilton and Barbra Streisand.

I didn't know that the American Cancer Society and The Salvation Army also held charitable events at the Paramount. In addition, the Society of the Arts, later to become The Society of the Four Arts, brought in symphony orchestras from Cleveland and Minneapolis for concerts.

I didn't know that the Paramount showed movies from 1927 through most of the 1970s until the last film, *Coal Miner's Daughter,* was shown on May 31, 1980.

I didn't know that the nude musical *Oh Calcutta* was performed live onstage to a packed house on February 17, 1978 in spite of a huge outcry of public opposition.

I didn't know that the Patio Restaurant, a prominent and memorable destination to many in Palm Beach, was located on the current site of the Paramount parking lot. In the later 1970s, it became the site of Trudy Heller's Nightclub.

I didn't know there was a citizens' "Save The Paramount" movement in the 1980s. More than 10,000 signatures were collected on a petition to "Save The Paramount."

I didn't know that the Paramount had been scheduled for demolition three times in the late 1970s and early 1980s, until the 1,236 seat interior movie theatre was converted to commercial office suites in 1985.

I didn't know that the Paramount was almost swapped for several acres of property on Palmo Way in 1980 and the town was going to move their administrative offices into the Paramount.

I didn't know about these *Palm Beach Daily News* headlines during the 1980s:

"Citizens Begin Last Minute Effort To Save Paramount"
"Curtain Closes on Symbol of Past Elegance"
"Doom Looms for Paramount Theater"
"Losing the Paramount Is Like Losing Part of PB"
"Time's Up For Paramount"
"Theatre's Gold Years In Shadow Of Wrecker"
"She's a Building That's Almost Sacred"
"PB's theatre needs miracle"
"Historic Palm Beach Theater To Be Saved"

And I didn't know that the Paramount had a very special place in the hearts of anyone and everyone who lived in Palm Beach during its years as a movie theater.

But then, what difference did it make?

The owners of the Paramount, the Resolution Trust Corporation, weren't going to rent to us anyway.

And they were selling the building.

DWIGHT, AGE 6

MY FATHER, JOHN "JACK" WINTHROP STEVENS, with my mother, Louise, in front of her father's General Store in Rosati, Missouri. 1940

**MY MOTHER, LUIGIA "LOUISE" ARGENTINA
RAMORI, born January 10, 1910 in Rosati, Missouri to
Peitro "Hector" Ramori (born 1880 in Bologna, Italy) and
Argentina "Nona" Vitali (born 1882 in Bologna, Italy).**

MOTHER'S BROTHERS & SISTERS, the Ramori family.
Standing: Ernie, my mother Louise, Nellie, Julia. Kneeling:
Dominic, Katie, Hector. Sister Inez took the picture.
1950

MOTHER'S SISTER, INEZ RAMORI PAULSELL, playing
the accordion. She was the second generation of accordionists
in our family. I am the third generation accordionist. 1930

GREAT UNCLE VICTOR HERBERT
PIAZZA, playing the accordion.

GEORGE BERNARD STARK, my gentle, well-mannered stepfather. "Pop" took on the responsibility of raising my brother and me when we were ages 14 and 8. He worked for the Terminal Railroad and took us all around the United States by train.

**WITH MOM AND POP in New York City during dermatology
residency at New York University Skin & Cancer Unit. 1975**

MY MOTHER LOUISE, age 95

Mother lived to be ninety-nine years and nine months.

MY BROTHER WIN STEVENS (far right) playing a round of golf with Jack Nicklaus (far left) at Frenchman's Creek Golf Course, Palm Beach Gardens, Florida. Also in the foursome were Bob Ave, chairman of the Board of Lorillard (second from left) & Harvey Rosenthal, president of CVS (behind Win). 1985

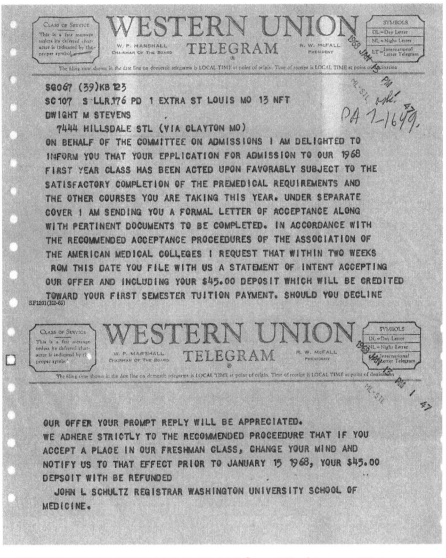

WESTERN UNION TELEGRAM from Washington University Medical School accepting me into their 1968 freshman class.

SOME OF MY ONE HUNDRED MEDICAL SCHOOL
classmates, class of 1972, at the University of Missouri
Medical School. I'm in the fourth row, third from left.

NEW YORK UNIVERSITY SKIN & CANCER DERMATOLOGY
residents, along with Chairman Rudolf Baer (standing, front
right) and Dr. A. Bernard Ackerman (seated front row, far
right). Dwight Stevens seated front row, far left. 1977

THE REV. DWIGHT STEVENS (far right) with his pastor since 1986, the Rev. Joseph Guadagnino, and his wife, Bea Guadagnino. 1995

FIRST MEDICAL MISSION TRIP to La Ceiba, Honduras, Central America. I brought my accordion with me to give away, but wound up playing it there for the first time in twenty-five years. 1988

DR. DWIGHT STEVENS WITH GURIFUNA CHILDREN in Santa Rosa de Aguan, on the northeastern coast of Honduras. This village was founded and inhabited by descendants of shipwrecked Africans in 1886. Grateful for our mission construction work, they prepared lunch for us every day ... one day it was iguana. 1990

WEARING PONCHOS GIVEN TO US in appreciation of our efforts, four members of our medical mission team, Hal Scott, myself, Winston McKen and Dr. Michael Reed, standing in front of our team transportation bus for the week in Riobamba, Ecuador. 1992

HAMMING IT UP ON HORSEBACK on medical mission trip
in the Andes Mountains village of Simiatuc, Ecuador, South
America. To get to this village, we had to travel three hours
and traverse a deep gorge. It was like going back in time – men
carrying holstered guns and riding around town on horses. 1995

THE REV. DWIGHT STEVENS with two Quechuan Indian children in the village of Pueblo Viejo in the province of Chimborazo during our 2014 medical mission trip to Ecuador.

MISSION TRIP DOCTORS: Dr. Dwight Stevens with Dr. Sandy Carden at La Mitad Del Mundo Equator monument just outside Quito Ecuador. We were given ponchos, hats and spears and a photo was taken with a background from the Amazon jungle. Our medical mission trip actually was up in the Andes Mountains at 11,000 feet altitude.
2016

HOWARD MINSKY, PRODUCER of the film *Love Story,*
the first person to tell me to write my story. 2006

THIRD GENERATION ACCORDION player, the Rev.
Dwight Stevens standing in front of the historical photographic
exhibit at the Paramount Theater building in Palm Beach.
2015

PARAMOUNT THEATRE, 1939, PALM BEACH, Florida.
Designed by Austrian architect Joseph Urban, the Paramount was
a dual-usage complex with shops and offices on the street and in
the courtyard, and inside a 1,236-seat movie theater. The film
Ice Follies of 1939, starring Joan Crawford and James Stewart,
was being shown. The Breakers Hotel is in the background.

Photo courtesy of The Historical Society of Palm Beach County.

**THE REV. DWIGHT STEVENS standing in the
pulpit of the Paramount Church sanctuary.**

39

West Palm Beach, Florida

"THERE SHE GOES. WAY BACK. IT MIGHT BE. IT COULD BE. IT IS," BELLOWED THE "Voice of the Cardinals," Harry Carey, broadcasting the St. Louis Cardinals baseball game.

Those words remain indelibly imprinted to this day in every Cardinal fan of the 1960s.

I was no exception.

Little did I know that one day they would help lure me to Florida.

Harry Carey brought baseball into our homes and backyards by radio. The games were almost overshadowed by his over-the-top exaggerated expressiveness, but he sure did make listening to a Cardinal game exciting and fun.

I often jokingly say there are two common threads that permeate and run through every person who is born and raised in

St. Louis - Cardinal baseball and Budweiser. And in my teenage years, the Cardinals were owned by the Busch Family, the makers of Budweiser.

Dr. John Kinney was luring me with the palm trees and beaches. But just as influential was my discovery that spring training baseball occurred in West Palm Beach, home of the Atlanta Braves and the Montreal Expos. Surely my beloved Cardinals would be coming over from St. Petersburg for spring training games.

As a teenager, I loved watching Stan Musial hit doubles off the pavilion screen at Sportsman's Park with my neighborhood friends Bob Meyer, Don Embree, Roger Marting, Dave DeVouton, Ron Williams and Steve Jennings. Lifelong friendships were cemented through our love-for-the-Cardinals bond.

We cheered together, watching Bob Gibson pitch another shutout and Lou Brock steal another base.

And we all had our collection of *baseball cards!*

I know the feverish passion for one's home team, whether it be baseball, football or basketball.

It is real.

It is ingrained.

It's still with me 50-plus years later.

If the Cardinals win, I feel better. If they lose, I don't feel so good. No longer do I even try to analyze or rationalize it.

No doubt every sports fan feels the same for their favorite home team.

I loved baseball and still do.

Like Harry Carey uttering his signature, "Holy Cow," I was thinking, *Holy Cow. Maybe I could meet Hank Aaron if I moved to West Palm Beach!*

The spring training facility in West Palm Beach wasn't the clincher in getting me to join John at the Palm Beach Medical Group, but it sure didn't hurt.

CHAPTER

40

West Palm Beach, Florida

IT WAS LIKE BEING AT A MINI UNIVERSITY MEDICAL CENTER.

That was what the practice of medicine was like with the Palm Beach Medical Group.

My first day, I'm in the same hallway as Dr. Kinney, my dermatology partner, and Dr. Ernie Jabour, one of the ob-gyn physicians. Just across the hall are two other ob-gyn doctors. Within minutes, internists, cardiologists, orthopedists, general surgeons, pediatricians and other specialists appear. There also was a pharmacy and a radiology department.

That is what I walked into.

The spectrum of physicians was truly remarkable. It was like being in a mini medical center, similar to, but on a smaller scale than, my residency at NYU.

I loved it.

My first patient had a skin cancer.

My second patient had a skin cancer.

My third patient had pre-cancers of the skin called actinic keratoses.

NYU Skin & Cancer had prepared me for this. Dr. Kinney and I worked together seamlessly and our NYU residency bond went deep.

Our practices were skin cancers, skin rashes, skin allergies and skin infections. Cosmetic dermatology was still years in the future. No injectable fillers in those days. And no lasers.

I loved going to the office every day. Just like Dr. Milstein. I never missed one day, except for one afternoon I went home early with a bad case of the flu.

This was my niche in medicine.

Or so I thought.

My fifteen years with the Palm Beach Medical Group can be divided into two parts - the eight years from September 1977 until June 1, 1985 and the ensuing seven years from June 1, 1985 to June 1992.

The Medical Group didn't change.

I changed.

My partners didn't change.

I changed.

The patients didn't change.

I changed.

The skin problems that I saw each day didn't change.

I changed ... in a variety of ways ... propelling me on a road to Doyle's office.

CHAPTER

41

North Palm Beach, Florida

"WHAT A DIFFERENCE A DAY MAKES," A SONG POPULARIZED BY DINAH WASHINGTON IN 1959 certainly applied to me.

Before June 1, 1985, the night when I was awakened with the thought in my mind, *"This pain will never go away until you turn your life over to God,"* I was a *fool*.

Yes, a fool.

Why do I say that?

Because before that awakening, I didn't believe in God.

Psalms 14:1 and 53:1 say: *"The fool says in his heart, 'There is no God.'"*

That was me.

There was no God.

There was no Jesus.

There was no faith.

I was a well-educated fool.

By June 1, 1985, I had a laundry list of accomplishments. Among them:

* graduated from Washington University in St. Louis with a Bachelor of Arts in Biology.
* received my Doctor of Medicine from Missouri University, where I also taught anatomy for two years, and completed six elective medical externships.
* completed a four-year internship and residency in dermatology at the world-renowned New York University Skin & Cancer Unit.
* practiced dermatology with the respected Palm Beach Medical Group for the past eight years.
* owned a three-bedroom house with a swimming pool, in-ground Jacuzzi, half-court basketball court and working stone fireplace that was custom installed for year-round use. The middle of summer? Just turn down the A/C to 65. It didn't matter that it was ninety-five degrees outside.
* drove a new 733i BMW.
* golfed as an eight handicapper with fitted woods and irons, custom made by Jack Nicklaus' personal club maker.
* shopped on Worth Avenue.
* engaged to be married, but more recently unengaged.

I was a thirty-eight-year-old *"fool."*

I didn't believe in God.

Slowly over the next seven years all that I had "accomplished" academically, professionally and personally diminished in importance.

Yes, *all!*

Why?

Because of the prayers of Muffy, Janet and Connie that reached the ears of our merciful and loving God.

> *"I revealed myself to those who did not ask for me;*
> *I was found by those who did not seek me."*

ISAIAH 65:1

That verse in Isaiah happened to me as God began to reveal Himself to me.

It would bring the first of many unexpected new acquaintances and friendships, even on the French Riviera.

CHAPTER
42

Nice, Cote d'Azur, France

"COME VISIT US ON THE FRENCH RIVIERA."

The invitation came from Ed and Maria Bacinich, patients of mine who were Palm Beach residents and spent their summers on the Cote d'Azur of the French Riviera.

And it came twice, once in 1984 and again in 1986 - one year before and one year after I became a Christian.

Debating about five seconds each time, I accepted their invitations ... both times.

Why not?

Ed was a brilliant physicist and an even more brilliant musician. Maria was an artist and the most entertaining person I have ever known. This was going to be fun.

Our friendship crystallized earlier in 1984 at the annual Greek Festival held at the Greek Orthodox Church on Southern

Boulevard in West Palm Beach. Ed was playing the bouzouki with the band and Maria and I joined the circle dancers. The ouzo was flowing.

And then their six-year-old son Todd cut his finger … deeply. No problem.

I immediately took him to my office and sutured his cut. It quickly healed. My emergency care cemented our friendship.

A few months later came the invitation to join them in the town of Villeneuve-Loubet, seventeen kilometers west of Nice.

The first trip was enchanting. We had breakfasts on the open-air patio of their Amiral condominium overlooking the Marina Baie des Anges (Marina Bay of Angels) on the Mediterranean Sea.

Lunch and dinner were at outside restaurants - either at the marina below or in Vieille Ville (Old Town Nice). Side trips to nearby Cannes, Saint-Tropez and to Cap d'Antibes Eden Roc Hotel filled our days with French cuisine, wine and laughter.

One day I set out by myself to explore the beach in Cannes.

My naiveté was quickly revealed.

Spotting a bikini-clad stunning woman in her mid-twenties, I thought I could overcome the language barrier with my charming personality and the early stages of a tan. I sauntered over to her. After about ten minutes of minimal banter and giggling, she gestured to the distant outside bar, requesting a cold drink.

Quick to accommodate, I set out to get the drink. It took about five minutes. When I returned, she was no longer there. I looked around and she was heading off arm-in-arm with a man three times her age. I watched as they crossed the street and entered the nearby hotel. It wasn't until later that day, when I saw a repeat performance, that the realization set in. It was my first experience with a call girl … and thankfully my last.

The 1986 trip brought an unexpected twist.

A friend of Maria's was also invited to visit them in Nice … an Astor … of the English Astors. Since she was about my age and single, Maria and Ed wanted me to meet her.

I was petrified!

This was about as far out of my social comfort zone as possible.

An Astor!

Of the Astor family of England.

What could we possibly have in common?

Virginia Astor's arrival was in the early evening. I was so reluctant to meet her that I managed to be out when she arrived.

When I girded myself for the intro, I sheepishly returned. To my utter amazement, Virginia and I hit it off right away and a lifelong friendship began.

I had become a Christian in 1985.

She also had recently become a devoted follower of Christ.

This was unexpected and a friendship was cemented … on the French Riviera.

Another young couple that I knew from my medical practice also happened to be in Monte Carlo at the time. The four of us jaunted around Monaco together, dancing in the nightclubs and touring small nearby villages.

This Lady Astor eventually married a McGillycuddy of the Reeks, a famous Irish ancestry hailing from the Reeks mountain range in County Kerry. His family lineage traced back to the year 300. Yes, 300!

I met her husband several years later, when they were living in France and I was on a mission trip to turn a chateau in Normandy into a Bible school and a church. While on that trip, I was invited to preach at a small, nearby church and I did. I spoke in English and Virginia translated for me in French. It was so special and so memorable.

The French Riviera became an imbedded memory, thanks to Ed and Maria Bacinich.

Through Maria and Ed, I met Virginia Astor. Without our mutual Christian faith, we never would have become friends.

More new friends and new experiences awaited, all because *I turned my life over to God.*

43

OH HOW I CHANGED. LET ME COUNT THE WAYS.

I was taken from a total non-belief in God, non-belief in Jesus Christ, non-belief in the Bible and zero church attendance to an absolute belief in God, belief in Jesus Christ, belief in the Bible and faithful church attendance.

I also was led to a thirty-one-year study of the Bible.

There were, of course, many gradual steps that resulted in these dramatic changes, all occurring *after* I invited Jesus Christ into my heart in 1985.

When I began to believe that there actually was a God, and that the Bible was a book that I had to learn and understand, slowly - very slowly - my thinking about what I was doing with my life began to change over the next seven years.

Yes, I had a dramatic experience in which my eyes and mind and heart were opened to God and to Jesus and to the Bible, but that *did not* take away my rationality.

It did not make me drop everything and become a medical missionary in developing countries.

It did not cause me to sell everything I owned and give it to a church.

But what did happen, gradually, is that God began to unfold a different course for me. It was a course that wouldn't negate my medical training, but would use that training in different ways.

The first change, which may not seem like much, was that *I began to be on time for my appointments.*

For me this was a big deal!

Patients had always been given a specific time for an appointment. But I, like most doctors, did not make much effort to see them at that scheduled time.

As everyone has experienced, it is not unusual to wait in a doctor's office for a seemingly infinite amount of time *until finally* being called into the inner office examining room area. It was no different in my practice. Patients were scheduled every ten to fifteen minutes. If they were seen within thirty to sixty minutes of that, no problem - to me.

That changed after I heard a sermon on Christians needing to be people "of our word," and that included being on time for appointments.

If one is late for an appointment, it shows a lack of respect for the person or persons for whom we are scheduled to meet at that certain time.

I was humbled and embarrassed by this simple truth.

I had not been respectful of those who were given a designated appointment.

It spilled over into my private life as well. I was *always "fashionably late"* wherever I went. *Always!* Seven o'clock to me meant 7:15 or more likely 7:30 … or whenever I got there.

That all changed.

But now, I believed that God was watching. Would I keep my word on a seemingly little matter of being on time for an appointment? This was the beginning of a principle I was being taught - to be faithful in small things.

It is a Biblical axiom that for bigger responsibilities to be given to an individual by God, one has to show faithfulness in small things. Maybe being on time isn't a big thing to many people, but for me it was. I had to show myself to be faithful to my word, every day, all day.

That was a big, big change for me!

And it carries over to this day in *all my appointments.*

To me, 6:30 now means 6:30 not 6:35.

Another change was that I began to offer to pray with some of my patients.

Boy did that cause some problems in the medical group!

After my own personal dramatic encounter with God on June 1, 1985 and subsequently experiencing first-hand miracles on medical mission trips, my zeal quickly outweighed my wisdom.

I was the typical caricature of a new believer in Christ. Everyone was going to hear about it, whether they wanted to or not. And I was going to offer to pray with everyone, whether they believed in it or not.

Since prayer wasn't the reason patients came to see me in my dermatology practice, there were complaints. The new medical director had the awkward task of telling me of the complaints. I could do nothing but sheepishly admit that I had overstepped boundaries.

The good news is that it gave me insight into when it is appropriate to share my faith and when it isn't. The inappropriate times easily outnumbered the appropriate times.

Prior to 1985, I recoiled when people tried to force their beliefs on me, whether Christian or otherwise.

There was one overzealous Christian whom I had hired to build shelving for me in my home. Whenever he would come to do the work, he would incessantly try to talk to me about Jesus. It didn't take long for me to tire of this - about fifteen seconds - and I fired him even though he was an excellent craftsman. I didn't hire him to preach to me.

The Bible tells us to "season our conversation with salt." Oftentimes that is just a pinch of salt. Any cook knows that too much salt ruins a recipe. The same is true with sharing one's faith.

Another change was that I began to keep a Bible open on the desk in my office. My desk was perpendicular to the doorway, so the Bible was easily visible walking by my office. And my door was almost always open. I would glance at the Bible between patients, a practice that kept my mind on spiritual things all day long.

An amazing thing happened one day when my eyes were opened to a world I had never seen before.

A cleaning crew came in every day after hours. One employee of this crew was a friendly African-American in his mid-forties named Fred. He and I would always say hello, but it never went beyond that.

When Fred noticed the Bible on my desk, he mentioned that he would like to learn more. I offered to meet with him and, one Saturday morning, he invited me to his home just off Palm Beach Lakes Boulevard.

The first time I went to his home, he and his wife graciously greeted me and invited me inside. It was a simple apartment. Fred and I sat in the living room, which had minimum furniture that had seen a lot of use.

As Fred didn't have a Bible, I explained some basics that I had come to understand. He enjoyed our session so much he asked if we could meet every week.

I agreed.

The next week I came with a second Bible and gave it to Fred. Our lesson lasted for about an hour and I noticed that

Fred never opened the new Bible. He just attentively listened and occasionally would ask for clarification.

It wasn't until the following week that I realized Fred couldn't read.

I was stunned, as I am today, that someone in the United States in their mid-forties, never had the opportunity to learn how to read.

We continued to meet every Saturday for more than a year. I taught Fred as much of the Bible as he could digest, without him ever admitting that he couldn't read it himself.

To this day, I am impacted by this experience with Fred. "There but for the grace of God go I."

Interestingly, in the seven years that I kept my Bible on my desk, not one of my medical colleagues ever mentioned it or ever expressed an interest in discussing Christianity, God, Jesus or the Bible.

Thankfully, and no doubt orchestrated by God, during those years between 1985 and 1992, into my office came Doyle Rogers.

The stage was being set.

And I had no idea.

44

INVITING JESUS CHRIST INTO MY HEART WAS THE PROPELLANT FOR ALL THE CHANGES that were to occur in my life. Being on time, offering to pray with patients and keeping a Bible open on my desk were just the beginning.

Major changes were coming.

But first I had to get a grasp of this Jesus.

I was going to church and hearing about this Jesus of the Bible.

Growing up, I had no idea who Jesus was. The churches I attended did not emphasize Jesus, nor did the pastors ever talk about sin or salvation or explain the Gospel of Jesus Christ.

In fact, crass as it may sound, the only time I remember hearing the name "Jesus" was when someone would hit a bad shot on the golf course. I would hear golfers emphatically, in exasperation or anger, say, *"JESUS!!"*

That was my only exposure to the name of Jesus.

For me, there was no historical figure Jesus.

He lived 2,000 years ago?

I never heard about him at home, in high school, college, medical school, internship and residency or medical practice.

What had I done in inviting Jesus into my heart on June 2, 1985, when Bill Hobbs took me to Maranatha Church?

Who was this "Jesus?"

What is this "New Testament?"

What and why is there an "Old Testament?"

I knew nothing about any of this, but soon it all unfolded.

Inviting Jesus into my heart on June 2, 1985 ignited something within me, something that can only be described as a spiritual awakening, a Holy Spirit awakening.

It's usually referred to as the "new birth" or the "born again" experience.

My spirit came alive for the first time when I invited Jesus Christ into my life.

The Holy Spirit of God came to dwell within me, changing me from someone spiritually dead to spiritually alive.

I was given a version of the Bible titled THE BOOK. This edition was written in layman's story form, like a novel. It was easy to understand, though later I found it's not as historically precise as other versions.

Several months later, I was given a New International Version Study Bible (NIV), a version for those who sought a more in-depth understanding of the Bible. It was more to my liking as it gave explanations of verses and passages with historical context.

Both THE BOOK and the NIV made sense to me.

The sermon messages made sense.

I began to meet "Christians" who, surprisingly, were sensible people.

There seemed to be something to this "Jesus."

And then I met the winner of the 1985 U.S. LPGA Open Championship. Little did I know that my love of golf would thrust me into a friendship that would soon set the course of my Christian life.

CHAPTER
45

Wellington, Florida

"IT WOULD BRING GLORY TO GOD," SAID KATHY BAKER IN RESPONSE TO THE TELEVISION interviewer's question.

It was July 13, 1985 and I was watching the third round of the 1985 LPGA Open Championship, played at the upper course of Baltusrol Golf Club in Springfield Township, New Jersey. A tall attractive blond named Kathy Baker, who had never previously won an LPGA tournament, was leading by one stroke ahead of Nancy Lopez and Judy Clark.

She was being interviewed on television and her response to the question, "What would it be like if you won?" caught my attention. Without hesitation she said, "It would bring glory to God."

It had only been six weeks since my life-changing June 1 experience when I was awakened in the middle of the night with the thought in my mind of *"Turning my life over to God."*

Her comment caught my attention.

I was glued to the television for the final round when she shot seventy and won by three strokes over runner-up Judy Clark (later Dickinson).

It was her first LPGA tournament win. And what a victory, the LPGA Open!

I wrote her a letter addressed to the LPGA, commending her public stand for God.

I never got a response.

A few months later, someone told me there was going to be a charity golf tournament in Wellington and many of the lady pros would be there, including Kathy Baker.

Golf was a passion of mine. Why not mix it with God? Seemed like a perfect fit to me!

I drove out to the Wellington event with the specific intent to meet Kathy Baker. In my pocket was a letter for her, commending her public expression of her faith in God.

That should get her attention!

Upon arrival at the Wellington golf course, she wasn't around.

I soon realized that in my urgency to get out on the golf course, I had forgotten to put on my golf shoes. I returned to my car in the parking lot, opened the trunk and proceeded to put on my golf shoes.

A white car came whizzing into the parking lot and pulled into the vacant parking space right next to me.

I looked over as the driver opened the door … and it was Kathy Baker.

With only one golf shoe on, I whipped out the letter in my pocket, thrusting it toward her and blurting out one of the inanest comments I've ever made in my life, "God wants me to give this to you."

She took the letter, looked at me and, without comment, quickly headed in the other direction.

I then tried to follow her around the course, with the hope of maybe talking to her. But it took me almost two hours to find her. I started on the front nine. She had started on the back nine. Finally, I caught up to her group and joined the gallery, which was maybe fifty people.

Once the round ended, the television interviewers surrounded her.

Once again she was talking about God … and this time she even mentioned Jesus.

I elbowed my way through to the front and managed to ask her where she went to church.

"Christian Love Fellowship in Deerfield Beach" was her answer.

That's all I needed to know.

CHAPTER
46

Deerfield Beach, Florida

IT WAS NOT UNTIL I UNDERSTOOD THAT I WAS A SHEEP THAT I REALIZED I NEEDED a shepherd. That occurred at Christian Love Fellowship Church in Deerfield Beach, when I began to be shepherded by the Rev. Joe Guadagnino.

The Bible likens people to sheep.

It's not a flattering comparison.

We're not likened to lions. Not to tigers. Not to bears. Not to horses. Not to any of the mighty animals of God's creation.

But to sheep.

To understand why people need a "shepherd" is to first understand and accept that we are figuratively "sheep."

This is not something many people are willing to admit, accept and act upon. The reasons are obvious and the parallels of humans to sheep are also obvious. And it takes true humility to accept them.

Sheep are stupid.

Sheep are habitual.

Sheep are stubborn.

Sheep cannot provide for their own food and they cannot lead themselves to fresh pastures to feed themselves.

Sheep tend to stray.

Sheep cannot defend themselves from predators.

Sheep are helpless, timid and easily scared.

Sheep follow the crowd.

Sheep cannot right themselves if they fall over on their back.

Sheep are restless.

Sheep will follow another sheep, even over a cliff.

Sheep are totally dependent on a shepherd to guide, lead, feed and protect them.

I gradually began to accept that *I was a sheep*, even though I was a well-educated professional. I was a doctor!

But I was still *a sheep*, even with my extensive resume.

I needed guidance about God, Jesus, the Holy Spirit and the Bible.

I needed a shepherd and Pastor Joe, as everyone called him, was willing to take on that role.

He was Kathy Baker's pastor, as well as pastor to several hundred others. For the most part, they all seemed to be reasonable, grounded, sensible and accomplished human beings who were excited about their Christianity.

Pastor Joe's church was fifty minutes one way from my home. There were services three times a week: Sunday morning, Sunday evening and Wednesday evening. In spite of the distance and although I was still practicing dermatology full time, I never missed any of them.

Even though I was a doctor, Pastor Joe treated me the same as he treated everyone else. My education didn't impress him. My profession didn't impress him. My titles didn't impress him.

What impressed him was my hunger to learn the Bible and to sit at his feet and listen as I slowly grew in my faith in God. He was always interested, available and accessible when I had questions or problems. And he still is to this day.

Pastor Joe knew God and he knew the Bible and I needed to learn from him.

He had something to impart to me, not me to him.

I was like a sponge, listening to his teachings and revelations about his understanding of God and the Bible. Just like in college or medical school, I took voluminous notes.

And he explained the Gospel of Jesus Christ.

CHAPTER

47

I DISCOVERED IT IS POSSIBLE TO GO TO A CHURCH AND NEVER HEAR THE GOSPEL.

Although I had been to "Christian" churches as a teenager, I had no idea what the Gospel was until I went to Maranatha Church in Palm Beach Gardens and Christian Love Fellowship in Deerfield Beach. And the Gospel is so simple.

I discovered that the entire New Testament is about the Gospel of Jesus Christ. But I also discovered that a knowledge of the Old Testament is essential in fully understanding the New Testament and the Gospel.

I learned that the Gospel is available for everyone, but it must be individually received. It is like a Christmas gift extended to someone. The person to whom the gift is given must receive that gift.

I learned the Gospel revolves around Jesus.

Who was He?

Who is He?

Who is He to me personally?

Jesus asked Peter that question in Matthew 16:15-16: "Who do you say I am?" Peter answered, "You are the Christ, the Son of the living God."

I came to believe that.

I also came to believe that I was a sinner.

What exactly does that mean in the 21st century?

Is sin really something that is contemporary? Or is that just some ancient Bible idea that has no relevance to our advanced civilization, learning and culture?

I had to understand "sin?"

I learned that the word itself implies "missing the mark." It means that I fall short of living each day on the highest, noblest plane of human behavior ... by word ... by deed ... by thought ... by motive ... by tone of voice ... by timing.

That just happens to be true. I fall short each day by word, by deed, by thought, by motive, by tone of voice, by timing.

And every day!

I learned that one attribute of the God of the Bible is that He is Holy.

And because God is Holy, He cannot have personal, intimate relationships with sinful people. A separation exists.

I learned that in the Old Testament, or Old Covenant, God required blood sacrifices for the sinfulness of people. This was called "atonement."

I learned that in the New Testament, or New Covenant, God Himself atoned for sin through the blood of Jesus.

I learned … and agree … that I am not *righteous* in God's eyes because of my sinfulness and there is *nothing* I can do to change this. Not enough professional accomplishments. Not enough charitable work. Not enough giving. Not enough loving. Not enough medical mission trips. Not enough degrees or honorary degrees. Not enough of anything.

But I learned that I can become righteous in God's eyes through what Jesus, God Himself, did to atone for my sinfulness. And *only through Jesus.*

I learned that this is the Gospel of Jesus Christ.

I also learned that receiving the Gospel of Jesus Christ is a starting point on a lifelong journey of changing, shaping and molding me into who God intended me to be.

I learned I must understand the Bible in its entirety for me to know and understand just what is pleasing to God and what is not pleasing to God.

I enrolled in a Bible college to find out what exactly is in the Bible.

CHAPTER

48

Deerfield Beach, Florida

SO WHAT IS IN THE WORLD'S BEST-SELLING AND MOST WIDELY-DISTRIBUTED BOOK?

I sure didn't know.

I'd heard people dismiss the Bible because it was written thousands of years ago. Others say it's difficult to understand.

I learned that there are sixty-six books in the Bible, thirty-nine in the Old Testament and twenty-seven in the New Testament. These two testaments are distinct but deeply connected. They tell one story, woven beautifully throughout all the books.

I learned that I could not possibly begin to understand the New Testament without an understanding of the Old Testament.

I enrolled in a Bible college in Deerfield Beach and attended classes in the evenings and on weekends for four years, even though it was a fifty-minute drive from my home. It didn't matter. What began as a fledgling Bible college in 1985 through the vision of the Rev. Dr. Joseph Guadagnino, South

Florida Bible College & Theological Seminary has grown to become fully accredited by the Association for Biblical Higher Education.

I was like a sponge during those four years, eventually getting a master's degree in theology in 1989 and a doctorate in theology in 1993.

"Theology" is the study of God. That's what the Bible is about and that's what I needed!

Although helpful, church sermons and Bible studies don't do what an intensive college study of the Bible will do. It opened up the Bible in so many new ways.

I took Old Testament courses.

I took New Testament courses.

I took courses in basic Bible doctrines.

But I found that taking these courses was not the end-all of Bible study.

The study of the Bible never ends. This was just the beginning for me, laying a foundation to build upon.

I discovered that the Bible is a book that "progressively reveals" itself to the reader. In time:

- More truths are revealed.
- More insights are given.
- More relevance is understood.
- More personal application occurs.

And it all comes with a greater and deeper personal understanding of God. I discovered the Bible explains who God is: His heart, His mind and His will. I so needed that, after years of being an atheist!

And I discovered the Bible explained who Jesus is.

I so needed that too.

I quickly found that the Bible is not a book that one reads through once and sets it aside. It is a book in which its verses and passages are personally and practically applicable to my life. One day, certain verses may apply to what is going on in my life. The next day, a different passage may apply, depending on the circumstances.

And that has never stopped!

I discovered the Bible provided a big picture of God's design and plan for the world. It even tells us how the world will end, what the days will be like leading up to that end and what awaits thereafter.

I discovered the Bible explains there is both a heaven and a hell after physical death occurs. It explains how to assure one's place in heaven.

A former atheist, I was becoming educated about the world's best-selling book ... and understanding what was in that book. This foundation was setting the stage for me to one day ask Doyle Rogers for his help in starting a church in Palm Beach.

But before I could even make an appointment to see Doyle, we were hitting roadblocks.

CHAPTER

49

"NO, NO, NO, NO, NO, NO, NO, NO, NO, NO, NO, NO, NO, NO, NO, NO, NO, NO, NO, NO, NO, No, No, No, No."

When the Resolution Trust Corporation refused to sign the lease at the Paramount, we found ourselves literally on the streets of Palm Beach looking for an alternative site. This was a daunting task because of the restrictive zoning requirements for a church assembly in Palm Beach, all of which were potentially met at the Paramount.

Over the next nine months, realtor Carol Digges and I were told "no" at twenty-six different places in Palm Beach.

Yes, a total of twenty-six.

Just *why* were we told "no" by each of these places?

Because the town required that the location must be zoned for a church assembly. We discovered there were very few of those in town.

Other potential problems: parking, fire code, handicap access, bathroom, traffic congestion and construction issues. They all must meet town code for a church. None are unreasonable, but each must be met.

We looked at each of the following locations, only to discover that not one complied for one reason or another:

Royal Poinciana Plaza
Royal Poinciana Playhouse
Palm Beach Public School
Palm Beach Day School
The Brazilian Court Hotel
The Chesterfield
The Breakers
Colony Hotel
Flagler Museum
… and seventeen other places.

At one point, Carol proposed we also could look on Flagler Drive. This was a realistic idea. After all, we were being told "no" everywhere we looked in Palm Beach.

But it seemed like each time a door closed for a possible location another possibility would immediately pop up. I was not ready to stop until we had completely exhausted every possible option.

We continued our relentless search, doggedly walking the streets of Palm Beach.

Then, after nine months of fruitless searching, *THE PHONE CALL* came.

50

"ARE YOU STILL INTERESTED IN STARTING A CHURCH IN THE PARAMOUNT?" WAS THE
question posed to me over the telephone.

I blurted out, "YES!"

Out of the blue, nine months after a limited partnership named Paramount Partners had purchased the building from the Resolution Trust Corporation, the managing partner of the new owners called me and asked if I was still interested in starting a church in the Paramount.

His next question was, "Can you come by to talk with us about this?"

No need to play coy here, I thought, and immediately said, "Yes. When would you like for us to come by?"

"How would tomorrow afternoon, around two o'clock, be for you?"

"OK. That works. I'll be there."

My thoughts started racing with the first glimmer of real hope. It had been a long nine months and the twenty-six "no's" were fresh in my mind.

The next afternoon, Carol Digges and I found ourselves sitting across a desk with the on-site managing partner for the new owners. His office was set up in one of the courtyard retail suites with just a desk, two chairs and a telephone. Aside from a few files on the desk, the office was barren. It was obviously a temporary office to meet prospective new tenants.

The managing partner began the meeting by saying he was aware that we had discussed a lease with the Resolution Trust. Unfortunately, the suite that we had originally looked at on the first floor was no longer available. It had been leased to another tenant. But they did have a larger suite available on the second floor if we would like to take a look at it.

He took us up to the second floor and we walked around the 1,818-square-foot, pie-shaped, centrally-located suite. I thought this might just work.

One drawback was that it was on the second floor, but it was easily accessible by elevator. We had been meeting in the Civic Association's second-floor office on Royal Palm Way for our weekly Bible study. No one seemed to mind that and there was no elevator, just stairs.

Floor-to-ceiling glass panels overlooked the atrium. It was a beautiful suite with an open, spacious feel to it and far better than the first-floor suite we had originally agreed to lease from the Resolution Trust.

But our nine months of rejections due to town codes for a church assembly had taught us to be thorough before we agreed to a lease.

Would this second-floor space comply with all town code requirements for a church assembly? We had to find that out before we pursued this any further. Specifically, would it meet the fire code requirements and how could we find that out?

My research on the Paramount could help us.

Through reviewing newspaper articles about the Paramount, I discovered that one of the owners, between 1980 and 1985, had plans drawn up to double the size of the entire building. The idea was to make the Paramount into a giant shopping mall by building a replica of the existing building in the parking lot. I recalled that there was a drawing of this plan in one newspaper article. The drawing was made by Palm Beach architect Gene Lawrence

Maybe Gene Lawrence's office would know if this second-floor suite would meet the fire code requirements for a church assembly?

I called his office.

CHAPTER
51

"IF I CAN HELP YOU, I'VE ALWAYS WANTED TO DO A CHURCH," GENE LAWRENCE TOLD US.

Gene Lawrence, the architect who had designed the plans to double the size of the Paramount, is telling me he's always wanted to do a church. He also designed the Sun & Surf and The Esplanade in Palm Beach.

I called his office inquiring about plans he might have from his proposed 1980s expansion for the Paramount. His secretary put me on hold.

The next thing I knew, Gene Lawrence was on the phone asking, "What are you doing at the Paramount?"

I told him we wanted to start a church and were looking at a suite on the second floor and wondering if it met the fire codes for an assembly. Maybe he might be able to tell us.

"Let me come over and take a look. How would tomorrow afternoon at three o'clock work for you?" he asked.

"That would be great," I stammered.

"I'll see you then," he replied.

The next afternoon, promptly at three o'clock, Gene Lawrence arrived at the Paramount.

He was fashionable in dress slacks, shirt, tie and sport coat. I learned that was his normal attire when meeting clients.

We looked around the second floor and he gave us some news we didn't want to hear.

"I don't think the floor or walls are two-hour fire-coded, which is required for an assembly in Palm Beach. And as the back walls are essentially glass, there really isn't anything we can do to improve that." But he graciously added, "If I can help you, I've always wanted to do a church."

He later told me that he had been retained to design a church chapel at Lost Tree Village in North Palm Beach. The project didn't happen and he was disappointed. Thus, he still had a yearning to design a church and see it built.

With Mr. Lawrence's assessment that the second-floor suite didn't meet town zoning requirements, we were back to square one.

I called the on-site property manager and told him the bad news. The second-floor suite just wouldn't work, although we greatly appreciated them calling us and trying to work something out. The next day he called me back with another offer.

"If you will move into the first-floor suite, just beneath the second-floor suite, we'll move the tenant that is presently in there to the second floor. Would you be willing to do that?"

Wow! I thought.

The first-floor suite was the prime location in the 30,000 square foot Paramount complex and it was 1,818 square feet, the same as the second-floor suite.

It was first-floor center, where the stage, screen and orchestra pit of the old theater had originally been located.

Dorothea's Dress Design Studio occupied the first-floor suite at the time. She also had a retail outlet in the front of the Paramount for her beautifully designed clothing.

I called Gene Lawrence back.

He came over the next day to look at the space.

"Yes, this will work," he said after looking around. "Let me know who will be your builder and let's do it."

I learned this was typical Gene Lawrence. He made decisions - fast.

Great! We had an architect. In fact, we had the best architect in Palm Beach!

It was all beginning to fall into place for me.

First, there was the original lease agreement that wasn't finalized at the Paramount.

Second, I was told "no" at twenty-six alternate locations.

Third, the phone call came *from* the new owners, wanting us to come to the Paramount.

Fourth, the second-floor suite not meeting code requirements led to the first-floor prime location suite being offered to us.

Fifth, Gene Lawrence, renowned Palm Beach architect, offered us his services *for free!*

This was all too much to pass off as coincidence or good luck. Too many doors were opening that I couldn't open myself.

It had to be God orchestrating everything. A foundation was being laid for the church to be planted in the Paramount, ostensibly by God's design.

Now we needed a general contractor.

Someone to work closely with Gene Lawrence and a builder.

Someone to oversee the entire project.

Someone with imagination.

A can-do type of person.

Of course, Richard Moody!

CHAPTER
52

"JUST CALL ME MACGYVER," RICHARD MOODY SAID LAUGHINGLY.

He half-jokingly would insist, "I'm a real-life MacGyver."

But he *could do anything, anywhere, anytime.*

There were no limits. Just tell him what needed to be done and he'd get it done somehow, someway.

The TV show "MacGyver," that ran from 1985 to 1992, featured the character Angus MacGyver as a secret agent. MacGyver would use anything around him to create solutions to any problem he faced. That truly was Richard Moody.

Richard and his wife, Jean, were regular attendees at my weekly Bible study. Both were devoted Christians and Richard had joined me on mission trips to Honduras and Ecuador.

There was a hospital in Trujillo, Honduras with so many holes in the roof that the operating room wasn't functional, because water poured into the overhead light fixtures.

"No problem," said Richard, as he arranged for roofing materials to be shipped to Honduras from the West Palm Beach port. Our team planned to spend three days repairing the roof. It only took two days under Richard's leadership. With the extra day, the team meandered around the hospital looking for things to do and discovered there was no running water.

"No problem," said Richard. He went into town, purchased 200 feet of PVC pipe and installed plumbing throughout the entire hospital. In one day.

And then there was the structure we built under his supervision on a sliver of an island on the north coast of Honduras called Santa Rosa de Aguan. This village had no communication with the mainland. If a structure was built, the government would provide radio equipment and they would be connected to the mainland for the first time.

Richard built that structure in three days. The concrete foundation was laid before we arrived and up went the concrete block walls, with windows and roof, all under Richard's guidance.

He managed to build it in Central America! In three days!

I saw him do it!

He was our man!

Richard knew I had been looking for a location for a church. When I told him that we were about to build a church in the Paramount with Gene Lawrence as the architect and we needed a building contractor, his response was predictable.

"No problem. I can do that."

There was plenty to do, pending our approval by the Palm Beach Town Council to renovate suites thirty-one and thirty-two into a church.

To Richard it was *all doable.*

The two suites needed not only a ceiling, as there were exposed pipes, but also fire-proofing, sprinklers, air conditioning ducts and lights. That was just the ceiling!

With Gene Lawrence's drawings, we envisioned an altar, the placement of pews and a wheelchair exit ramp with a railing.

"Can all these things be built?" I asked.

Of course, his response was "no problem."

He suggested that we hire Zammit Corporation Builders, known for their expert carpentry work, and Carpenter Electric. Together they would finish the ceiling, build a sound booth, install ceiling lights, wall sconces, wall speakers and a recessed video projector with a drop-down screen.

When I introduced Richard to Gene Lawrence, there was an immediate natural chemistry between these two can-do men. It was fun for me to watch.

They did it all, right before my eyes, just like Richard had done in Honduras.

All we needed now were two things: Town Council approval and furnishings.

No problem!

CHAPTER
53

Deerfield Beach, Florida

THEY WERE ALL SINGING JOYFULLY, SOME WITH THEIR HANDS LIFTED UP.

What are they doing?

This is a church!

The congregation was standing at Christian Love Fellowship Church. Almost everyone was singing loudly. Some were swaying to the rhythmic music. Some had their hands lifted up like they were waving to someone.

This would go on for ten, fifteen, twenty, even thirty minutes. Sometimes longer. No one was clamoring for it to stop. The people were loving it.

Occasionally a service would *just be all singing. The whole service!*

There were live musicians playing musical instruments - electric guitars, trumpets, electronic keyboards and even a drummer. Sometimes a flute or violin would join in.

The words to the songs were projected onto large screens for the congregation to see. No one looked down at printed pages. There were no hymnals. They all were looking up.

This was light years away from what I had seen and experienced in churches when I was a teenager, where we sung from hymnals.

There also were soloists with beautiful voices. But for the most part the attendees of the worship services were doing the praising and worshipping … themselves.

The music was upbeat at times and, at times, soft and reverent.

I liked it.

Nobody complained that there was too much singing. If anything, it seemed some wanted to sing more and have it continue longer.

This was my introduction to contemporary *Praise and Worship.*

And this was my introduction to the longest book in the Bible, the Book of Psalms.

I soon learned that the Book of Psalms is a songbook. It is longer by far than any other book in both the Old Testament and the New Testament. That in itself told me something about God's attitude towards music.

The Psalms repeatedly say to sing joyfully and to do this accompanied by a variety of instruments, including trumpet, harp, lyre, tambourine, strings, flute and cymbals (Psalm 150).

This was all new to me. Very new!

But I found it to be based on biblical verses. That was all I needed to accept this new and different kind of music in a church setting.

I have come to believe church worship isn't meant to be exclusively a spectator event, but something which we, as individuals, do. We sing *TO GOD* personally, even if we are part of a congregation that is worshipping. I never knew that growing up.

I discovered great moving songs in hymnals with deeply profound lyrics. But I found that if I am "looking up" while singing rather than "looking down" at words written in a book, it is easier for me to focus my thoughts on God.

I found that some "older folks" dismiss contemporary music, thinking it isn't spiritually deep enough. All songs, even the oldest hymns, were once considered "contemporary." I learned not to dismiss contemporary music if it ministers to people's hearts and minds.

Experiencing the music of the '50s, '60s, '70s and '80s, church music with those kind of rhythms move me just as much, if not more, than hymnal music.

I found that the *"lifting up of hands"* while worshipping God in song is also found in the Bible (Psalm 28:2; 63:4; 141:2). It can be a sign of reverence to God, exalting God or even an expression of surrender to God.

The Bible also says to *sing with joy to God* and even to *shout with joy* (Psalm 66:1; 81:1; 95:1; 98:4; 100:1).

I discovered that because one doesn't sing well does not excuse anyone from taking part in the worship. If the singing is from one's heart, God hears and God approves of worshipful singing, regardless of pitch and skill.

Singing to God is wonderful.

It is something I have learned.

I found the last verse of Psalm 150 says, *"Let everything that has breath praise the Lord."*

Well, that includes me. I'm still breathing.

And I have come to love singing to God, whether in church, at home or even in my car.

But singing praise and worship songs was not the only thing that took hold of me from this new life of going to church.

Something else was birthed within me. Something I never would have imagined.

CHAPTER
54

Honduras, Central America

"WHY WASN'T I BORN IN A VILLAGE LIKE THESE PEOPLE IN HONDURAS WHO LIVE IN cardboard boxes on the side of a river that floods every year with the monsoon rains?"

This was a question I asked myself after returning from my first medical mission trip.

"Next time you have a mission trip, I'll go along and we'll have a medical clinic also," I innocently said to Todd Dwyer, our church missions director.

Like many churches, Pastor Joe's church did mission trips. As I sat in the congregation listening to the team members' report after their return from Honduras, I politely listened, but had no real interest. It was nice what they were doing, but I had other things on my mind - like a 1:30 p.m. tee time with some golfing buddies.

Then one day, an idea popped into my head. The next time they take a mission trip, I'll go along and hold a medical clinic. After all, I was a medical doctor!

It was that simple.

And that naïve.

In 1988, a team of ten from our church went to Honduras.

I was the only physician.

Thankfully, there was a retired American doctor, who was living there with his Honduran wife. He did the clinic with me … or rather I did the clinic with him. He was experienced in developing world medicine. I wasn't.

Over 400 people showed up for this four-day clinic in the sweltering August heat and humidity. They lined up and waited for hours and were amazingly grateful for anything we could give them, even a small bar of Holiday Inn soap.

The medical problems were endless and serious: skin infections, intestinal parasites, chronic bronchitis, cancerous growths, gastritis, congenital deformities and broken bones that had never been set correctly.

It was heartbreaking for me to see the extent of years of untreated disease and it opened my eyes to developing-world conditions, where oftentimes people have virtually no medical care.

These people who came to our makeshift clinic literally lived in cardboard boxes on the side of a river. And when the river would flood each year, their "village" would be washed away and they would have to find another riverside location to set up their transient "homes."

It was so beyond belief for me that this was their life.

No hope for betterment.

No hope for education.

No hope for anything.

Just existence. And a hard, hard existence.

What struck me *very hard* was my return to the Miami Airport.

I looked around and became uncomfortably conscious of the air conditioning, the electric lights, the men's and women's bathrooms, the drinking fountains and the food concessions.

Traveling back home on I-95, I noticed the white lines separating lanes on the highway. In Honduras, we saw few paved roads and those that were paved had endless deep potholes. There were no white dividing lines. There were no lanes!

A startling thought came to me, *"Why wasn't I born in that village of cardboard boxes on the side of a river in Honduras?"*

I had no answer to this.

Why was I born in the United States?

With an opportunity for education.

Why was I born white, admittedly an advantage in the U.S?

What had I done to merit these advantages, compared to the people I had just given the most minimal medical care at an improvised clinic in the sweltering heat and oppressive humidity of Honduras?

For months this bothered me.

Why was I given these advantages?

My life wasn't exceptional compared to many born into privilege. I wasn't born into a "silver spoon" family. There was no trust fund. I never knew my father. But I had a home provided for me, meals provided for me and clothing provided for me. Study opportunities were available to me through college scholarships and medical school loans.

Then on to New York City to a world-renowned dermatology residency. And then to south Florida, working for a private medical practice, driving a new 733i BMW, living in a three-bedroom home with my own swimming pool, an in-ground Jacuzzi, a custom built-in stone fireplace and bottled water delivery each month.

Compared to Honduras, my life was *excessively luxurious!*

And it all started with my birth in the U.S.

Why was I allowed to be born in the U.S. with all the inherent advantages?

This *unfairness* continued to trouble me until I found a scripture passage in the Book of Acts 17:26, which God "... *determined the times set for them and the exact places where they should live."*

This realization put everything into a new perspective for me.

The sting of the blight of life in a cardboard box on the side of a river has never left. But the understanding came to me that it was God who determined that I was born into my family in the U.S. and given the accompanying opportunities for education.

What came to me then, and has never left me is, "To whom much is given, much is required."

With the advantages I have been given, God has an expectation: *"Dwight, what will you do with these advantages and privileges I gave you?"*

My response has been simple, humble and grateful: keep going on these mission trips, offering whatever skills I have and enlisting whomever might want to go along.

That's the simple story of my medical mission work. I have been given a lot and I must give back.

Another memorable trip to Honduras was to Santa Rosa de Aguan, a sliver of land on the north coast, inhabited by Garifuna Indians. They were descendants of African slaves who had shipwrecked off the coast and settled on this island. We built a small structure for use as a radio station. They were so grateful they made lunch for us one day … iguana.

These mission outreaches from Pastor Joe's church were in conjunction with a Bible school in La Ceiba, Honduras. Another outreach was in Quito, Ecuador at Cristo Al Mundo, also a Bible school. Pastor Joe was invited there to teach and he asked me to accompany him.

There I met another doctor.

CHAPTER

55

Quito, Ecuador, South America

"I GO TO ANDES MOUNTAIN VILLAGES ON HORSEBACK TO SEE PATIENTS," SAID DR. Bacilio. At least that is what I think he said to me in Spanish.

The year was 1989 and Pastor Joe had invited me to accompany him to teach at Cristo Al Mundo.

This particular evening, I was standing in the back of the room because, literally, hundreds of local students had come for these evening Bible classes. Some came with the hope of becoming a pastor. Some came just wanting more in-depth understanding of the Bible. Some just came for spiritual feeding.

A man stood next to me. He was neatly dressed in plain black slacks and a gray, long-sleeve shirt. His shoes were black. He was shorter than me. He was darker skinned than me. His hair was jet black. He seemed to always be smiling.

He was Inca Indian-like in his facial features.

My four years of high-school Spanish and attempts to communicate with Hispanic patients at Bellevue Hospital during residency was about to be tested to the max when I was told he was a medical doctor.

He spoke no English.

I managed to engage him in a conversation that was more gestures than words.

Yes, he was a doctor.

A medical doctor.

I wondered what he did as a medical doctor in Quito.

"Que tipo de medicina hace?" I asked, "What type of medicine do you do?"

"Voy a las montanas, para ayudar la indigena," he answered. "I go to the mountains to help the indigenous."

That was a conversation stopper.

I didn't have a follow-up question for that response.

"Viajo por caballo a los pueblos," he volunteered. "I travel by horse to the villages."

This was beginning to get interesting.

"Quiere venir conmigo?" he asked. "Would you like to come with me?"

"Interesting question," I muttered in English.

It was time to get a real interpreter.

With one of the staffers who was fluent in Spanish functioning as an interpreter, we sat down and began to talk.

I learned he was a Quechuan Indian, the descendents of the Incas of South America. He had been born in a mud hut in a village four hours south of Quito.

He was the fourth Quechuan to become a medical doctor in the history of the country. The other three had moved into the bigger cities where people were more affluent. He was the only one who was determined to go back and help his own indigenous people in their mountain villages.

I looked at this man.

He was sincere.

He was genuine.

He was not asking me for money.

He was a committed Christian, as was his wife. He had two children, a son and a daughter, both under the age of five.

His name was Bacilio Malan Guacho.

The last name of "Guacho" is a Quechuan Indian tradition, adding on the wife's last name to the husband's last name.

I said, "I will help you," having no idea how I could possibly do that.

Within a year, I returned with a medical team. There were ten of us, three of whom were medical doctors and seven were lay people.

Within two years, I returned with another team. This time there were twenty-eight of us, including two from WPTV-Channel 5, a West Palm Beach television station. Station manager Bill Brooks wanted to film a documentary on what we were doing.

Our teams went into mountain villages. I never knew what awaited us in these villages. Dr. Bacilio planned everything, but it was before email and he had no telephone.

We brought medicine from the U.S. Some were donated by St. Mary's Hospital and some were over-the-counter meds from Costco, which included vitamins, ibuprofen, antacids, eye drops and Tylenol.

Our medical clinics are held in schools or churches. People line up hours ahead of time and patiently wait all day to see an American medical doctor.

They dress as native Quechuans, wearing colorful red, blue, green or purple ponchos. And they all wear hats, even the ladies, who carry their small infant children in woolen slings on their backs.

Examinations are always a herculean task. It is cold in these mountain villages and the people wear endless layers of woolen clothing.

In these clinics, most of the children have intestinal parasites from the impure water.

Most adults have half their teeth and the remaining half are decaying.

Together, we eventually built a medical building from the ground up in Riobamba, where Dr. Bacilio sees patients year-round and has learned to do cataract surgery.

A man born in a mud hut does cataract surgery!

When I'm there, I look around at the majesty of the Andes and see terraced farmed mountainside, painstakingly worked by hand. The colorful dots in the distance are people carrying the produce of their fields up and down the hillsides.

Peering out of the jeeps or busses as we journey to the villages, I see horses, cows, sheep, mules, bulls, llamas, vicugnas, hawks, goats, pigs, roosters and the occasional wolf. And when we stop, once in a while I see hummingbirds dancing among the wild flowers.

The broken glass on the walls around homes and buildings always catches my eye. The glass is strategically cemented in place during construction as an attempt to ward off intruders, reminding me this is a developing country.

To my amazement, so many of the Quechuans love God and love Jesus.

They may not have much in terms of worldly possessions, but they possess a faith that is strong and sure.

That is all part of why I keep going back.

They are part of the family of God, my brothers and sisters in Christ living in mud huts.

CHAPTER
56

Deerfield Beach, Florida

"ANYONE HERE WITH SINUS TROUBLE, THE LORD WANTS TO HEAL YOU TONIGHT. COME down to the altar," was the declaration from visiting guest minister the Rev. Dr. Bob Lemon.

I sat there, almost in the back row of the church auditorium, and thought about the past three years of misery I had from sinus trouble. Three different doctors, one otolaryngologist and two allergists, had not solved the repeated sinus infections that I experienced shortly after moving to Florida.

I thought, *"What do I have to lose? Should I go forward? This was preposterous!"*

I found myself standing up and slowly proceeding down the aisle towards the altar. What did I have to lose?

On the way to the altar my sinuses cleared up, miraculously!

My breathing was normal instantly!

Rev. Lemon never prayed for me.

He never laid hands on me.

He never anointed me with oil.

God had miraculously touched me and healed my sinuses, *on the way to the altar.*

That was twenty-nine years ago and since then I've only had one episode that subsided in a week one year ago.

The Bible is replete with stories of miraculous healings that Jesus performed. The book of James says if anyone is sick, that he or she should call upon the elders of the church to pray for him or her and be anointed with oil (James 5:14).

This *all* stands in stark contrast to my teachings in medicine, my life's profession.

Yet, time after time through the years, I have witnessed the healing power of God through prayer or a miraculous divine touch to myself or to others.

I also have prayed for people's physical healing and nothing has happened and have seen others prayed for and healing *did not* occur.

My first experience with God's healing power - when *I* prayed for someone - occurred on my first mission trip to Honduras. It was the last day of the trip and some of us were still in the remote clinic we had set up for the hundreds of local people. All the elder ministers and the one other physician had gone back to town and we were finishing up our work in the sweltering clinic.

A forty-something-year-old woman with no front teeth came, asking us to treat her children for intestinal parasites. We gave her the medicines they needed. She then told me that she had stomach pain.

What should I do? I'm a dermatologist!

The general medicine doctor had left and there were no phones to call him.

All I could recall from my medical school days was that I should examine her abdomen. I had her lie down and, in the right upper quadrant of her abdomen, I felt a tennis-ball-size, rock-hard tender mass. She flinched at just the slightest touch to that area.

There was nothing medically we could do, so we prayed.

My pastor's son, Tony Guadagnino, was with us. He and I gently placed our hands on the mass. Another five or six members of our team circled around us, all laying hands on this woman. We prayed for God's mercy. After ten minutes, the mass was half the size.

I didn't say anything. I just looked at Tony.

He looked back at me.

We were both speechless, our eyes wide open. We didn't know what was happening.

We continued to pray.

In another fifteen minutes, the mass had totally disappeared in our hands!

The woman jumped up, waving her hands to the sky and praising God! Then she left the clinic with her children.

We all sat there, too amazed and too awestruck at what we had just witnessed.

On my return to the Palm Beach Medical Group, I described the case to a gastroenterologist. I asked what the mass could have been, but didn't tell him what had happened. He said without hesitation, "That's cancer of the colon."

All I know is that we had nothing to offer this woman medically. We prayed and the mass totally disappeared. She knew it and she praised God!!

On my second trip to Honduras in 1990, a twenty-year-old waif of a girl was carried limply in the arms of her father into the Bible school where we were teaching. He had laboratory documentation with him showing that she had leukemia, with white blood cell counts over 100,000. The doctors told him there was nothing that could be done. She was dying.

We laid our hands on this emaciated, seventy-pound girl and prayed for her.

The next year, when we returned with another mission team, this same girl was healthy, vibrant, walking, running and talking. Her blood counts were normal.

It could only have been the healing power and mercy of God!

I, myself, have had a few medical issues since.

In spite of prayers and being anointed with oil, twice I've had to have operations. The first surgery was for varicose veins in my left leg, probably the result of running high-school track and cross country in addition to years of standing as a doctor. Another time was for an inguinal hernia, the result of lifting a heavy potted plant.

Prayer did not resolve either of these.

But in 2006, I was diagnosed with chronic lymphocytic leukemia. Through prayer and an over-the-counter nutritional supplement called AHCC, my white blood cell counts - which had risen to 55,000 - are now in the 20,000 to 30,000 range. I've never had a symptom and never had to have any medical treatments. I still see an oncologist every four months. At my last visit a few months ago, my oncologist said, "It's a miracle."

I still believe in medicine, medical doctors, medical technology and medicines and I still have an active medical license.

I also believe in praying for people.

It is up to God what happens after that.

CHAPTER
57

Palm Beach, Florida

I HAD TO TELL DOYLE THAT IT WAS H. LOY ANDERSON'S IDEA FOR ME TO START A CHURCH in Palm Beach.

During those last years of private practice, I had become friends with H. Loy Anderson Jr., who was a patient of mine at the Palm Beach Medical Group.

H. Loy, also known as Harry Loy, epitomized Palm Beach: wealth, charm, privilege and charisma. He exuded likeability, was everybody's friend and a natural born leader. How that friendship began is a remarkable story.

I was walking through our waiting room one day and happened to notice a Palm Beach businessmen's magazine. Out of curiosity, I flipped through the magazine and was surprised to see a lengthy article about Harry Loy Anderson Jr. His father had been a banker in Palm Beach and Harry Loy had followed in his footsteps. He had become president of a bank. The article was primarily about banking. But Harry Loy also openly talked about Jesus and how Jesus had changed his life.

This couldn't be true!

It wasn't possible!

He was talking about Jesus?

This was not the Harry Loy I knew!

But it was true.

After reading the magazine, I called him up and asked him if it was true that he had turned his life over to Jesus. Just as he did with everything else, he exuberantly, emphatically and openly told me, "Yes, it is true!"

Like a doubting Thomas, I needed to see this for myself to believe it.

I asked him if we could get together, because I also had turned my life over to Jesus three years ago. He said, "Sure, let's have lunch together."

We did and I found that he had genuinely become a believer in Jesus Christ and a devoted churchgoer. He even hosted a Bible study in his bank every Thursday morning. At times others would lead this study, but Harry Loy was the catalyst. People came because he had so many friends and was so well liked.

We became friends as brothers in Christ.

In time, he came to know my story and my dramatic change from atheism to my belief in God and in Jesus. I also shared my vision for starting a church in Palm Beach County. I told him of the many significant changes that happened to me in the medical group since June 1, 1985, paving the way for this career change. He continually encouraged me to start a church.

But some things had to happen first.

They did.

CHAPTER
58

West Palm Beach, Florida

"ACCEPTING MEDICARE ASSIGNMENT IS AN ETHICAL ISSUE," I SAID TO MY ASSEMBLED medical group colleagues.

After coming to believe in the Gospel of Jesus Christ, enrolling in Bible college, taking annual medical mission trips, experiencing the miraculous disappearance of three years of sinus infections, playing the keyboard in church and offering to pray with some of my patients, something was destined to give professionally.

And what gave was harmony with my medical colleagues.

It came to a head at one of our monthly medical group business meetings.

Attendance at these business meetings was not mandatory, but most of the doctors attended. My participation was always limited, as I never had much interest in administrative matters. The group hired people to handle that.

At the time of this meeting, there were no limits to what we could charge a patient. We set our fees and the patient's insurance usually covered some, but not all, of our fees. The patient was responsible for the remainder.

When Medicare came along, it drastically changed things as Medicare was now setting fees for medical services.

The choice was either to accept Medicare assignment – the "reasonable fee" that Medicare sets for office visits and procedures - or not accept the Medicare assigned fees.

When this topic came up on the agenda, I did something I had never done before. I stood up, walked to the front of the assembled group of thirty doctors and gave a two-minute impassioned argument that we had to accept Medicare assignment.

This was so uncharacteristic of me.

But I believed this was an ethical issue that needed to be decided *as an ethical issue.* We should be thinking of the patients *first.*

I knew that many of our patients were on fixed incomes. It would not be right to bill them whatever we wanted. They just didn't have the resources to pay the overage above whatever insurance covered.

After my two-minute speech, I returned to my seat in the back and sat down. One person clapped. Dr. Marty Thomas. All the others remained silent.

The discussion went on for another two hours. I said nothing more, but listened to my colleagues talk about the financial impact of accepting Medicare.

Finally, they took a vote.

The majority voted in favor of accepting Medicare assignment, based on it being the best financial business decision for the group. The rationale was that if we didn't, we would lose patients and therefore lose business.

No one mentioned that it was an ethical issue.

As I drove home, I felt as lonely as I have ever felt.

No one listened to me or shared my reasoning.

It bothered me immensely that my colleagues didn't see the issue as I did. Not one of them thought it was an ethical issue. I felt like a lone voice in the wilderness … like a salmon swimming upstream against the current.

I felt an uneasiness with my colleagues that I had never felt before. This continued through the night and was still with me when I awakened the next morning.

What was I doing in partnership with these other doctors?

They saw things so differently than I now did.

At that stage of my new faith, I was just learning that prayer was two-way communication with God. It was more than just me talking to God. I was being taught to give God the opportunity to "talk" to me also. This was new … and strange.

That morning, after I had spoken my prayers, I lay down and silently waited, not knowing what I was waiting for.

As I lay there quietly, what came into my mind was a specific thought. There was no audible voice, just a clear concise thought: *"It's my approval that counts."*

I lie there stunned, but cracked a smile.

An assurance came over me that although my colleagues didn't understand me or endorse my position, someone else did understand and endorse what I had done ... God Himself.

At that point, I was not even familiar with the Scripture verse:

*"Am I now trying to win the approval of
men, or of God? Or am I trying to please
men? If I were still trying to please men,
I would not be a servant of Christ."*

Galatians 1:10

My short presentation was delivered with the right motive, thinking of the patients first, not how it would affect our financial interests.

That was pleasing to God.

And that was the first time that I became aware of a dilemma I would repeatedly face in the future - the dilemma of pleasing people or pleasing God.

That "Medicare assignment issue" was a turning point for me, setting the stage for my future. I didn't make a decision at that time to stop private practice, but it was apparent that my future wasn't going to be with my colleagues. We thought too differently.

A few other nudges in that same direction were soon to follow.

CHAPTER

59

Lauderhill, Florida

"*TITHING! JOHNNY MILLER, YOU ARE DUPED,*" I THOUGHT WHILE WATCHING A GOLF tournament on television in 1986.

People who know golf know Johnny Miller or know about Johnny Miller. Winner of two U.S. Opens, Miller shot a scorching eight-under sixty-three in the final round to come from six strokes back of Arnold Palmer to win at Oakmont in 1973.

Johnny Miller was a golfing legend.

I had seen Johnny Miller hit a golf shot, up close, fifteen feet directly in front of me during his astounding run of stellar golf in the 1970s. He was playing in a PGA Tour tournament at Inverrary in Lauderhill and I followed him around for a few holes.

He was about 175 yards away to a slightly uphill green and, although I was behind the ropes, he was right in front of me.

He hit a five-iron like I have never seen a five-iron hit before or since.

Like a bullet it pierced the air, right at the flag, landing softly five feet from the cup. I was left open-mouthed, not only by the trajectory of the shot, but also by the sound of the shot. It hit as flush and crisp as a golf ball can be hit. Wow!

A few years later, he was playing in a tournament that was televised. In an interview, he mentioned that he *tithed* his winnings to his church.

I was aghast!

How could he be so duped?

To me, this was another absurdity of "religion," in which people are manipulated to give money … like to TV preachers who promise tenfold and hundredfold financial returns.

Ridiculous!

Then I began to hear teachings on tithing and read the scriptures on tithing. One-tenth of income *is* to be given to the "storehouse," where one is being spiritually fed.

It took several years for me to accept this, but it was clearly a Biblical principle.

I grudgingly began to tithe, writing checks for ten percent of what I earned as a doctor. It was substantial, I thought.

I did not do it gladly. In fact, the opposite was true. But I did it obediently to the Scriptures.

The principle became indelibly imprinted on me, *personally,* a short few months after I began to tithe to my church.

About two years previously, a prepaid medical plan was established in our medical group and all the doctors were given the opportunity to participate. We each put in $1,800 and essentially *owned* this health plan. Participation was voluntary.

I decided to participate.

Two weeks after I began to tithe and was writing those painful checks of ten percent of my gross income, one of my partners told me that our prepaid health plan had been purchased by a national organization. We had been bought out and each of us would receive a percentage of the negotiated purchase price.

I didn't think much more about it. That's fine, I thought.

Then the check came a few days later in the amount of $110,000!

I laughed.

Why?

Because the timing was right after I began tithing.

The Book of Malachi states that until one *tithes,* God has blessings stored up in heaven that He cannot bestow unless one tithes:

> *"Bring the whole tithe into the storehouse, that*
> *there may be food in my house. Test me in this,"*
> *says the Lord Almighty, "and see if I will not throw*

open the floodgates of heaven and pour out so much
blessing that you will not have room enough for it."

MALACHI 3:10

I learned that tithing is the *only principle* in the Bible in which we are to *test God*.

Through the years, I discovered that not many Christians avail themselves of this opportunity and consequently keep themselves from all of God's blessings.

It has to be said that if one tithes with the motive of getting money back, God sees right through that. It won't work. The motive is wrong. Tithing is simply being obedient to the Scriptures. God will determine what "blessings" He has in mind and they *might not be financial*.

Receiving that check for $110,000, from which I tithed $11,000 to my church, allowed me to pay off the mortgage on my home and pay off my car, eliminating all my debts at the time.

Having no debt made my next decision much easier.

CHAPTER

60

I HAD TWO CHOICES: SIGN THE NEW MORTGAGE OR RETIRE FROM PRIVATE PRACTICE.
The choice was easy.

In 1990, I had verbally given notice to the medical group that I was intending to leave the next year. We had recruited another dermatologist and he would fill my position. Then the Gulf War started and the new dermatologist we recruited happened to be in the naval reserve.

He was activated for duty.

And just like that he was gone.

For at least a year.

"OK," I said. "I'll stay on until he returns."

That took more than a year. Meanwhile, another significant development occurred.

Columbia Hospital entered into an agreement with the Palm Beach Medical Group to buy the building, owned by the group, at 7th Street and Olive Avenue. A stipulation of the agreement was that the group must relocate and build a new building next to the hospital on 45th Street.

Another stipulation: the doctors must sign onto the mortgage for the newly-built medical building.

I couldn't do that.

My priorities had changed.

My life goals had changed.

I was now teaching a Bible study in my home.

My thoughts were in the embryonic stages of entering the ministry in some way.

Signing a long-term mortgage just wasn't in the cards for me.

When the time came to sign onto the new project, I declined.

I actually made this profession-changing decision based upon the Bible.

A passage in 2 Corinthians 6:14-17 basically told me what I must do:

"Do not be yoked together with nonbelievers ... 'come out from them and be separate, says the Lord.'"

My colleagues and I were now in two different worlds, *because I had changed.*

I couldn't sign onto that long-term mortgage with my colleagues and be "yoked" with them.

I chose to leave the medical group with literally no place to go, though I was left with four possibilities.

I could enter the full-time ministry. I was debt free. But no church ministry opportunity presented itself.

I could open a new dermatology private practice by myself. That would entail a huge financial outlay for equipment and staff.

I could, perhaps, join another dermatologist in private practice, if I knew another committed Christian dermatologist.

I didn't.

Or maybe, just maybe, I could work for the Palm Beach County Health Department as a dermatologist.

But that sure would be different than private practice.

61

THE FISHING KIT FROM SPORTS AUTHORITY SEEMED TO BE JUST WHAT I WOULD NEED.

I had just "retired" from the Palm Beach Medical Group and had time on my hands. I thought, *Maybe I could offer my service to the health department?*

For the past few years, I made an arrangement with the Palm Beach County Health Department to send their dermatology patients directly to my office at the medical group and I would see them.

I set specific time slots - 10:30 each morning and 2:30 each afternoon - for health department patients. They came almost every day and sat in our waiting room along with the other private patients. Miraculously, no one complained, as these were - without question - the downtrodden in our county.

When I inquired with the health department if they needed a dermatologist on staff, they invited me for an interview.

"Could you start dermatology clinics at our various locations in Palm Beach County Monday through Friday?" came the question from the head of the health department.

"Maybe. What exactly does that mean? Where would I go?" I asked those questions without having a clue as to what lies ahead.

"Well, we have clinics in West Palm Beach, Riviera Beach, Lantana, Delray Beach and Belle Glade," was the answer. "You could go to each one of them once a week for a half day. We pay $30 per hour."

They're asking me to drive all around the county to get to their clinics. I was accustomed to a fifteen-minute daily drive to the medical group. Lantana, Delray Beach and Belle Glade would be thirty minutes to an hour, one way.

"OK, I can do that," I found myself saying.

It just seemed the right path for me. Taking care of indigent patients every day, people who had little or no access to medical care, would be just like one of my mission trips. I didn't care about the minimal salary. It would pay for my gas.

I had my own surgical instruments for biopsies and small procedures.

How could I bring them with me?

Maybe in a fishing kit.

Sports Authority came to mind. There I found the perfect piece of equipment. It had four pull-out drawers and a lift-up top. I could store instruments, bandages, gloves, local anesthesia and syringes. I'd be a traveling doc.

It worked.

For the next twelve years, I went to those five different clinics in Palm Beach County … and one more.

After the first five years, the Riviera Beach clinic, which was a pediatric clinic, closed and was replaced by an HIV Clinic. Every patient was HIV positive and that's where the real serious pathology occurred. With lowered immunity, skin infections went unchecked. It was a real challenge. And I would triple glove every time I performed a skin biopsy.

I gasped seeing a patient with shingles. It was infinitely worse than the worst case in a person with a normal immune system.

Another time a patient came in complaining of itching. On examination, he had small bumps all over his body, including his face and scalp. Itching and skin bumps were common in patients with HIV, but this just looked different. I took a skin biopsy.

It *was different.*

Unbelievably and fatally different.

The biopsy showed cutaneous cryptococcosis, a potentially life-threatening fungal disease that had disseminated through the patient's body.

I had never seen a case like this, not even at NYU, a world referral center for rare diseases.

He wasn't ill. He was just itching. Upon receiving the biopsy report, we immediately had him hospitalized. The disease had spread to his lungs and brain. He died within a week.

The health department experience was grueling and humbling, but I felt privileged to do it.

As these health department clinics were just half a day, I had some extra time on my hands. I was already leading a weekly Bible study in my home and I began to look for a location to start a church.

My thinking was that patients had come to see me from as far north as Stuart, as far south as Fort Lauderdale and as far west as Belle Glade.

Central Palm Beach County is where I should look. Probably somewhere close to the medical group in downtown West Palm Beach.

It didn't turn out that way.

CHAPTER

62

"I'VE NEVER BEEN TREATED MORE RUDELY. I DEMAND A CONFERENCE CALL," CAME THE message to me from my nurse.

I smiled … for several reasons.

I even began to laugh.

My retirement from the medical group was just a matter of a few months away, so my perspective had changed. I'd probably never see this patient again after today. The Palm Beach County Health Department most likely was where my professional future will be.

But I was laughing primarily because I knew her story. And *she* wasn't to be taken seriously.

This woman had been a lounge singer who hit the jackpot and became one of the most publicized, photographed women in Palm Beach.

All because she married into money and position ... *BIG MONEY and BIG POSITION.*

She came to my office that day after experiencing an allergic reaction to medication. Her regular dermatologist, my partner, was away on vacation and she begrudgingly accepted the appointment with the junior doc.

But not without a fight.

After I entered the examination room with my nurse, the former lounge singer demanded that my nurse leave immediately. However, our office policy was that when seeing female patients, I always had a nurse in the room.

She emitted this command from a standing position ... actually more a standing *posture.*

She didn't *sit* in a doctor's office.

She *stood* in a doctor's office.

Dressed in sartorial powder-blue splendor, she could have come from a Vogue cover shoot, resplendent in her custom-tailored pantsuit with matching powder blue stiletto heels.

Her hair and nails were perfect, no doubt a daily ritual performed by some indentured servant.

It was obvious she had one or two face lifts as she approached the big five-o.

She wore a pearl necklace with matching pearl earrings and a pearl bracelet.

Her diamond ring, that flashed its brilliance, was large enough to cause momentary blindness from its reflection if the light was just right.

As it was 2:30 p.m., she most likely had just come from a gala-planning luncheon. The "committee" is made up only of ladies who plan *The Big Event*, while not-so-subtlety checking each other out from head-to-toe for designer labels, jewelry, accessories and recent plastic surgery.

I said "no" to her command that my nurse leave the room.

She reiterated her demand, this time with a fierce snarl attached to her words. I didn't know that someone could snarl in English with a French accent. I learned that day it is possible.

She *did not see a doctor* with a nurse present.

I again, politely as possible, explained that it is office policy that I always see female patients with my nurse present.

At that, she glared at me. She no doubt would have bolted out the door with ingrained histrionic fanfare had her skin problem not been so severe that it required this *"emergency appointment!"*

We faced each other, like two lions on a plain. One was going to win. One was going to lose.

She knew it.

I knew it.

I didn't care if she bolted out the door.

I held all the cards.

She had the skin problem.

I was the skin expert and her regular dermatologist servant, my partner, was away for another week.

And she couldn't possibly tolerate for another moment the annoying severity of the allergic drug reaction.

She sneered, huffed, puffed and glared at me with well-practiced daggers that had caused most others to wilt under that stare.

I didn't.

After what seemed like hours of silence, I knew she had relented. She had to. She was just too miserable.

My nurse stayed.

We then got to the root of her allergic reaction. I solved it for her.

She left without a "thank you."

I simply was glad she left.

The next day came *The Call*.

My nurse stopped me in the hallway between patients. The lioness was on the phone and was demanding a conference call. She told my nurse that she had never been treated so rudely.

I told my nurse to ignore the call and tell the lioness I was with patients.

She didn't call back, but no doubt gave my partner an earful upon his return.

Ah ... the women of Palm Beach.

Well, not *ALL* the women of Palm Beach.

Many are lovely, kind, mannerly, educated, polite and pleasant. And then there are the demanding, haughty tyrants. They usually were graced by God with good looks and a sense for fashion, which helped them land a rich husband.

I was accustomed to a tyrant in my midst.

My mother was that way.

She ruled.

Everyone submitted.

Except for me and my brother. We both stood up to her and either said "no" or we just didn't tell her what we were doing.

Although the lioness and I never crossed paths again, for which no doubt we were both thankful, little did I know that within a few short years I would be coming to her turf ... Palm Beach.

CHAPTER
63

Palm Beach Gardens, Florida

"CAN YOU TELL ME ABOUT JESUS?" I INNOCENTLY ASKED THE MINISTER AT MARANATHA Church six months after I said the prayer to invite Jesus into my heart.

I was attending church services three times a week and people were saying *"I Love Jesus"* and there were songs about Jesus, but I had no idea who Jesus was.

That may seem far-fetched, but from the churches I attended growing up, I never knew who Jesus was. And now, ministers are talking about *"Jesus said this in the Gospel of Matthew"* and *"Jesus said this in the Gospel of John."*

What were they talking about?

There were these terms flying around: Lamb of God, Son of God, Savior, Lord, the Word, the Good Shepherd, Redeemer, Mediator of a New Covenant, the Way the Truth and the Life, the Bread of Life, the Messiah.

They not only said *"Jesus,"* but *"Jesus Christ."*

And "Jesus" was coming back a second time!

This was all new to me.

What were they talking about?

I soon discovered that virtually everyone had an opinion about Jesus and answers varied from Teacher, to Prophet, to Rabbi, to part of the Trinity, to the Son of God, to Lunatic, to the Christ.

So ... who is Jesus?

Who *was* Jesus?

Why is He referenced by so many different terms?

And what do all these terms mean?

My quest to grasp the meaning of all these terms began to unfold the more I read my Bible.

I found that my New International Version Study Bible mentioned "Jesus" approximately 1,274 times in the New Testament. There are another 543 verses in which "Christ" was mentioned and 98 verses about the "Gospel."

"Who is Jesus?" was posed by Jesus Himself, in Matthew 16:15-16 when He pointedly asked this very question to Peter: *"Who do you say I am?"* Peter's response was, *"You are the Christ, the Son of the living God."*

My study led me to even more questions.

Is Jesus the Lamb of God to me, the one who took away my sin by the sacrifice of His blood on the cross?

Is Jesus my Savior? Am I a sinner in need of a savior from my personal sins?

Is Jesus my Lord? Is He master of my life?

Is Jesus the Good Shepherd to me? Have I acknowledged that I am figuratively a "sheep" who needs guidance, protection, feeding and leading?

Is Jesus the way to eternal life for me with God after death?

Is Jesus the Messiah to me? Is Jesus the Christ to me, the one predicted in the Old Testament over three hundred times, fulfilled in the coming of Jesus?

Did I believe in the *"Gospel of Jesus Christ?"*

I didn't even know what the *"Gospel of Jesus Christ"* was.

CHAPTER
64

"MATTHEW, MARK, LUKE AND JOHN." IS THAT A SINGING GROUP?

I had never been told that these four guys were authors of the so-called "Four Gospels."

When I first heard about them I thought, Matthew, Mark, Luke and John sounds like a folk music group ... kind of like Peter, Paul and Mary.

No one bothered to tell me that the word "gospel" meant "good news." That I had to find out for myself.

So I started reading Matthew.

The introduction in my Bible says Matthew was a tax collector. He was considered a traitor to his own Jewish people, a quisling, an unethical opportunistic businessman and one who should be avoided.

This was *the author of this first book of the New Testament?*

The author of the second book, Mark, wasn't much better. It seems he was a young man who bailed out on a missionary trip with Paul and went back home, causing a rift between Paul and Barnabas.

Things started to improve with the third gospel when I discovered Luke was a physician, although I wondered what kind of medicine they had two thousand years ago. My first thought was that *he couldn't have been all that effective.*

I recalled from TV westerns that doctors in the Wild West had little to offer their patients except whiskey when they were taking out a bullet from a high-noon shootout. And that was just a few hundred years ago.

Then I remembered that the father of medicine, Hippocrates, lived in the fourth century B.C., so maybe Luke had some additional knowledge and skills by 30 A.D.

The last guy was John. Everybody seemed to insist that if one starts reading the Bible, his gospel was the place to start.

I quickly saw that John was a big-picture kind of guy, a deep reflective thinker and passionate to the point of being nicknamed "Son of Thunder."

What's the "good news" these four guys supposedly wrote about? Apparently, it was that Jesus came to earth and died from His crucifixion on a cross.

I thought, *"That's good news?"*

It wasn't making much sense to me and these four guys were so different from one another that they probably would not have spent any time with each other socially.

I decided this needed a deeper look.

Matthew it seems was a bit of a scholar, even though his occupation was exacting tax payments. I found that some call his book "The Swinging Door," the perfect connection between the Old Testament and the New Testament.

Mark exudes the enthusiasm of youth. Action, action, action fills his book. No discourses. No deep introspection. Just eye-popping tales of Jesus. The only thing missing is WOW! POW! BAM! BONK! SMASH! ... kind of like the soundtrack from a Batman series.

Luke says that his book is a careful investigation to prove the certainty about Jesus' life versus the fiction. His book is replete with historical accuracies. Obviously, he did his research.

John begins by calling Jesus "the Word" and saying that Jesus was "with God in the beginning" and that Jesus "was God."

A pretty strong statement to launch his book.

John knew Jesus better than anyone and he knew not only what Jesus said but what Jesus meant.

In describing Jesus as "the Word" he was saying that Jesus was the mind of God, the thinking of God, the heart of God.

And John emphasizes that Jesus came to earth with specific purposes in mind, the most important being "eternal life."

And the necessity of a spiritual birth.

To John, a miracle was never just an isolated act but a window into the reality of the spiritual Kingdom of God.

I pondered these four very different fellows.

They had four widely different personalities and four very different viewpoints of Jesus.

Was there anything that they had in common?

It was evident there was something.

They each believed in, and were followers of, Jesus Christ.

As I thought about this, it became clearer to me that the choice of these four guys from very different backgrounds shared the bond of belief in Jesus Christ, which overrode all superficial differences. That seemed to me to be a very significant ingredient of what is called the "good news" ... *the gospel is for everyone.*

But I needed a better understanding of this.

CHAPTER

65

"JUST LOOK UP SCRIPTURES THAT MENTION GOSPEL.

It will all become clear to you then," came the well-meaning advice.

Sounds logical, I thought.

It can't be that hard.

I started, like Luke, to meticulously and carefully investigate "the gospel."

I found 277 verses that contain the word *"gospel."*

That's **two hundred seventy-seven!**

In the New Testament!

The fog began to clear as I began to grasp some theological concepts, the first being that the blood of Jesus Christ was sacrificed for sin, bringing forgiveness of sin to all who receive this free gift from God.

Sounded fine.

But blood?

Sin?

Forgiveness?

Still a bit murky to me.

I learned that an attribute of the God of the Bible is that He is holy, meaning God is separate from everything that is sinful and evil. There is no trace of sin or evil in our holy God. He is transcendently separate and pure. He is perfect, whereas humans are imperfect.

For people to dwell in the presence of a holy God requires the removal of sin. And I, as a sinner, am powerless to do that on my own. There is nothing I can do, give or buy to accomplish that.

Yep, I came to understand and believe that I am a "sinner."

Never thought about that before.

Never was told that before.

Never considered that before.

I learned that *"sin"* is simply "missing the mark." Or more practically, it means that I do not think or behave on the highest, noblest plane of human existence every day, all day, by thought, word, deed, motive, tone of voice and timing.

I readily have to admit that I don't.

And that defines me as a "sinner," like it or not.

I found that the book of Romans addresses the principle of forgiveness of my sin by the shedding of Jesus' blood. This leads to what is called a *"righteousness from God"* (3:21-24) through faith in Jesus Christ.

It is so simple.

The fog began to clear as I came to understand that the "good news" *is* that *my sins can be forgiven through Jesus Christ.*

That is basically *"the gospel."*

It is so simple.

And it is freely offered to all. But, like every gift, it must be *received individually and personally.*

I received it.

I began to think that this *gospel is paramount!*

I know that is a play on words, but the gospel is of *supreme importance!*

In addition to this concept of the gospel, my Bible tells me not only how the world began, but how it will end and where people will wind up. That too is of *paramount importance!*

I began to look at the last book in the Bible, for that is where I found understanding of what lies ahead for everyone and *why the gospel is so important.*

66

YIKES! THE BOOK OF REVELATION! WHAT'S THAT ALL ABOUT?

I hear plenty of predictable reactions when the "Book of Revelation" is mentioned. Especially from Christians, who often respond with a deer-in-the-headlights stare coupled with a comment usually reflecting confusion, fright and an admission that the book is indecipherable.

Non-Christians also have a blank deer-in-the-headlights stare, but for a different reason. To them, the book is totally foreign, except for maybe having seen an apocalyptic magazine cover referencing the book. Needless to say, the book is dismissed as having nothing to do with their reality.

Yet, I found that the Book of Revelation is without a doubt the most revealing of *God's overall plan for the entire world and all of mankind.*

Now that says a lot!

What is so difficult about this book? The first five words of chapter 1 explain what it's primarily about: *"The revelation of Jesus Christ."*

That tells me something.

And everything!

The book's theme is *Jesus*. It says so in the *first five words of the first chapter.*

The key to unlocking this so-called mysterious final book of the Bible is to grasp the meaning of the title word *"revelation."*

How simple is that?

I looked it up.

"Revelation" is the English translation of the Greek word *apokalypsis,* which means *unveiling.*

OK. Unveiling of what?

Simple.

An *unveiling* of Jesus Christ, which was not revealed previously in either the New Testament or the Old Testament.

There are some hints in both testaments, but that's all, just hints.

The gospels, the Book of Acts and the New Testament Epistles tell us:

* that Jesus existed before all things.
* that He came to earth birthed by the Holy Spirit through Mary.

❧ that He was on the earth for thirty-three years.

❧ that He was crucified.

❧ that He died on the cross.

❧ that He was resurrected from the dead.

❧ that He was taken up to heaven before multitudes of witnesses.

❧ and that He sat down at the right hand of God, interceding for saints.

And the gospels say that Jesus will return a *second time.*

That's about it.

I began to look for *new ways* which Jesus was *unveiled, uncovered* or *revealed* in Revelation.

Chapter 1 gives the first *new unveiling* of Jesus in John's vision in verses 13-16. He sees Jesus in His glorified heavenly state.

"… someone 'like a son of man,' dressed in a robe reaching down to his feet and with a golden sash around his chest. His head and hair were white like wool, as white as snow, and his eyes were like blazing fire. His feet were like bronze glowing in a furnace, and his voice was like the sound of rushing waters. In his right hand he held seven stars, and out of his mouth came a sharp double-edged sword. His face was like the sun shining in all its brilliance."

This image of Jesus is not seen before in the New Testament.

This is the *living Jesus in heaven!* A far cry from the crucifixion.

I found a second *new unveiling* of Jesus in Chapters 2 and 3, in which He not only is depicted as the *head of the church,* but the one who carefully and incisively evaluates His churches.

I found a third *new unveiling* in Chapters 4 and 5, where Jesus is depicted as the only one qualified to "open the scroll" of judgment about to befall the earth for its wickedness.

What follows is a detailed depiction of what is called the Great Tribulation in Chapters 6 through 18. Many Christians find this section alarming. I found it to be "good news" that believers in Christ will be spared this end-of-times judgment by God on the ungodly, the unrighteous, the wicked and the evil of the entire world.

But that's not all!

A fourth *new unveiling* of Jesus comes in Chapter 19 where Jesus' second coming is depicted. He is a warrior King triumphing over *all the forces of evil* in the world. This is a startling contrast to the crucified Jesus of the gospels.

The last *new unveiling* is found in Chapters 21 and 22, where those whose names are written in the Lamb's Book of Life (21:27) will dwell *with God and Jesus* in a new heaven, a new earth and a new Jerusalem.

Wow!

That's how this earthly experience will culminate.

It's nice to know the future but I have to live in the here and now!

Let's talk about that.

CHAPTER

67

IT ALL STARTED FOR ME, IN THE HERE AND NOW OF THE PAIN OF HEARTBREAK, AWAKENING at 4 a.m. on June 1, 1985 with this thought in my mind ...,

> *"This pain will never go away until you turn your life over to God."*

I came to realize this out-of-the-blue thought had two parts:

1) *"This pain will never go away until ..."*
2) *"... you turn your life over to God."*

I had absolutely *no idea* what any of that meant at the time.

"Turning one's life over to God" was as foreign to me as moving to the Sudan.

Only one person had said that to me two years before, my friend Bill Hobbs. Thankfully that gave me a starting point.

The *"pain will never go away"* - did not immediately catch my attention as much as the *"turn my life over to God."*

But God did heal the pain of my broken heart and many years later I found four Bible passages that address the *"brokenhearted:"* Psalm 34:18, Psalm 109:16, Psalm 147:3 and Isaiah 61:1.

God did take away that pain *and* He even restored the broken relationship.

And God made me forget the pain of my distress and the days, weeks and months of my distress, just as He did for Joseph (Genesis 41:51-52).

I have found that God brings me relief from any and all of my painful or disappointing life experiences and God understands me far better than people do

In turning my life over to God I began to experience His love, a new and different kind of love.

CHAPTER

68

PAUL WROTE ABOUT LOVE MORE THAN ANYBODY ELSE?

Wasn't he the same guy who was breathing out murderous threats against the Lord's disciples?

And wasn't he the one determined to wipe out that heretical sect of Jesus followers?

And now he's talking about *LOVE?*

Can't be the same guy!

You say he changed?

How could someone so intelligent, so accomplished, so special by birth into the tribe of Benjamin, an exemplar keeper of the Pharisaical law and zealous for legalistic righteousness, come to say everything was meaningless compared to knowing Jesus?

He said he was acting out of ignorance and unbelief?

That was a little hard to digest!

He even considered himself the worst of sinners, a blasphemer, a persecutor and a violent man.

I found that after Paul's experience with Jesus on the road to Damascus he wrote about *love* in every one of his epistles.

Yes, *love.*

A unique kind of love, translated from the Greek word *agape,* which is defined as *unconditional* and independent of the actions, thoughts or attitudes of another.

I learned that this was God's love for me.

Unconditional.

Paul put it into a perspective that emphasizes just how important this *agape love* is to God in 1 Corinthians 13:

> *"And now I will show you the most excellent way.*
> *If I speak in the tongues of men and of angels, but*
> ***have not love,*** *I am only a resounding gong or*
> *a clanging cymbal. If I have the gift of prophecy*
> *and can fathom all mysteries and all knowledge,*
> *and if I have a faith that can move mountains,*
> *but* ***have not love,*** *I am nothing. If I give all I*
> *possess to the poor and surrender my body to the*
> *flames,* ***but have not love,*** *I gain nothing."*

1 Corinthians 12:31b - 13:4

What a perspective!

I couldn't help but notice that many things held in high regard in Christian circles are listed: spiritual gifts, knowledge, understanding, faith, giving and even martyrdom.

Paul says that although these might be good and of value, without them being expressed with love, they are nothing … in God's eyes.

I imagined it as if one would have a conversation with God saying, "God, I was able to trust you by faith for miracles."

And God replies, *"Are you rude?"*

Or, "God, I gave millions of dollars to my church and to charitable causes to help less fortunate people."

And God says, *"Do you keep a record of wrongs?"*

Or, "God, I teach the Bible and understand the deeper spiritual principles of the bible."

And God says, *"Do you boast?"*

Paul came to understand that in God's eyes things are different and I came to understand that too.

I have asked myself, "Is being *loving* more important than a ministry?"

I concluded the answer is *"Yes."*

I have asked myself, "Is being *loving* more important than being pastor of a church?

I concluded the answer is *"Yes."*

I have asked myself, "Is being *loving* more important than taking medical mission teams to developing countries?"

I concluded the answer is *"Yes."*

To God, *love is paramount.*

And this kind of love, from God, is something that is absolutely unique.

I mess up. I make mistakes.

But, in spite of *all my shortcomings*, I have come to realize that God still loves me.

There might be consequences from my mistakes. I might have to make amends for what I say and do.

But God still loves me.

Paul understood God's love and it changed his whole perspective on life and gave him a whole new and different purpose for his life.

Although my encounter with God wasn't as dramatic as Saul's on the Road to Damascus, God got my attention and changed the course of my life.

Thank God!

Paul also came to know that God had a "race marked out for him."

I began to wonder if there was a *"race marked out"* for me.

CHAPTER
69

Palm Beach, Florida

DOYLE BEGAN TO FLIP TROUGH THE PAGES OF MY PORTFOLIO AND I BEGAN TO TALK.

"It was suggested to me by H. Loy Anderson that I come to Palm Beach to start a church."

I noticed he was listening, even as his gaze focused on the pages of the portfolio.

"I asked thirty-three people from Palm Beach what they thought of the idea and thirty-one of them thought it was a good idea. The list of those people is in the section titled 'People.'"

I noticed he turned to that section and his eyes widened as he read the list. He knew most of them.

"Gene Lawrence will be the architect of the project." This caused him to look up directly at me. He knew Gene.

Now he was really looking at me. He also knew Hal Scott. Both he and Hal had been past presidents of the Civic Association.

"There is a list of topics I've been teaching at the Bible study in the section 'Bible Study Topics.'" He turned to that section and was obviously now beginning to become interested.

"We have a lease agreement at the Paramount for a suite on the first floor, contingent upon Town Council approval. We were told that we will need both a special exception and a variance from the council. This came from a meeting with Dave Zimmerman and Harry Ackerman of the Building and Zoning Department. The lease agreement is in the section titled 'Lease' and the town requirements are under 'Town.'"

He didn't comment, but he turned to that section and read it in its entirety.

I stayed quiet until he looked up.

"The realtor who helped us obtain the lease, Carol Digges, is president of the Palm Beach Board of Realtors," I added.

"There is a drawing of the suites that we will be renting in the section 'Paramount.' Gene Lawrence made those drawings for us." I wanted him to see exactly where we were planning the church in the Paramount.

"We've incorporated the church and have a tax-exempt application ready to file. That is in the section titled 'Legal' and Ernst & Young will be our accountant," I said, hoping that he would realize this was all for real.

He continued to thumb through the portfolio and I waited.

He then said, "I didn't know you had a degree in theology, were an ordained minister and are now working for the Palm Beach Health Department. That's admirable."

Those details were on the same page of the portfolio that also showed St. Mary's Hospital had placed me on the emeritus staff and Good Samaritan Hospital on the honorary staff.

He raised an eyebrow and commented about the newspaper article from March 11, 1991, in the *Palm Beach Post's "PEOPLE TO WATCH"* section about me.

"I like the last comment you made," he said. "'It's not what's on the outside of a person that's really important, but rather what's on the inside.'"

I just smiled.

He closed the portfolio and looked right at me.

"I'm impressed," he began.

"It seems like you've done your homework and you have a lot of good people helping you."

"Yes, there are a number of people who have been helping and encouraging me to do this," I managed to say.

He paused, pressed the fingertips of his hands together in front of him and said, "I'll represent you before the Town Council."

CHAPTER

70

EVEN WITH DOYLE ROGERS AND GENE LAWRENCE BY MY SIDE, I STILL FELT INTIMIDATED walking into the Town Council chambers.

It was December 14, 1993 and we were on the agenda of the monthly Palm Beach Town Council meeting. As we waited our turn to be called, if I could have paced the halls I would have. It was that nerve racking for me. Doyle and Gene sensed my anxiety. They were experienced pros at this and both assured me it would all go well.

Around the semicircular polished wooden dais, raised eighteen inches above the rest of the chamber, were eleven jet-black executive leather chairs. There sat the mayor, the five-member Town Council members, an alternate, the town attorney and town administrative employees.

Behind them were paintings of eight previous mayors, the largest painting being that of Capt. E. M. Dimick, mayor from

1911-1918. He loomed right in the center, behind the dais. He appeared to watch all the proceedings below with a fixed gaze, glancing a bit to the right.

I thought it was an appropriate gaze, as Palm Beach has always been more than a bit "conservative."

In front of the dais was a four-foot white colonial balustrade, which visually enhanced the separation of those in authority and those in the audience.

Police Chief Joseph Terlizzese and town employees, including building and zoning officials, sat in the audience.

An attorney would amble forward to one of two podiums and present the client's case to the council. It was a time-tested procedure.

Everything was recorded and transcribed.

It was all very formal.

Our case was called.

Doyle stepped to the podium on the left and presented our case, requesting a special exception for the church to be allowed in the 1,818 square-foot area in the Paramount. He advised that the name Paramount Church had been chosen because it would be located in the Paramount building.

The staff was asked for comments.

They had no objection.

A motion was made by President Pro Tem Hermine Wiener to grant the special exception.

The motion was seconded by Lesly Smith.

On roll call, the motion carried unanimously. President William Weinberg and council members Nancy Douthit and Michelle Royal all cast "yes" votes.

It was all over.

In less than five minutes, the Town Council gave us approval to start the church in the Paramount.

I let out a sigh of relief and thanked Doyle and Gene.

Wow!

A monumental step forward had occurred.

To me it was huge. For Doyle and Gene, it was just another Town Council meeting.

With the approval to go forward, all we had to do was renovate the dress design studio into a church sanctuary, find some pews and have church services.

The pews came from an unlikely source.

CHAPTER

71

West Palm Beach, Florida

THE ABANDONED METHODIST CHURCH IN CITIPLACE WAS THE UNLIKELY SOURCE OF OUR eighty-year-old oak pews, thanks to David Paladino.

"You can have the pews as long as you have a church," David said to me. All we had to do was to figure out what might be salvageable.

Within a few days, Richard "MacGyver" Moody and I peered into the abandoned church. It was now a huge musty place, with termite infested pews. But they would be ours if we wanted them.

As I went from pew-to-pew, it was evident that most were collapsed and beyond repair. The particle dust from termites was piled up in large mounds and seemed to be under every one of the sagging oak pews and communion rails.

Were any of these salvageable?

How was Richard going to tackle this? I thought.

"No problem," Richard said, predictably.

This can-do man came up with another can-do idea.

"We'll move the pews into a rented moving van. Then we'll have the van tented to kill the termites," he said.

"Sounds like a reasonable idea," I said.

I called Tomasello Pest Control, explaining to them what we wanted to do. Coincidentally, Blanche Tomasello had been a patient of mine at the medical group. They were willing to go along with Richard's termite annihilation plan.

We rented a large moving van and Richard enlisted some young men to move approximately thirty, seven-foot sections of oak pews into the van. Some communion rails, bolted to the floor, were taken up and placed in the van alongside the pews.

Right on schedule, Tomasello arranged to tent the moving van overnight to kill the termites.

It worked.

With the help of an antique restoration business on Dixie Highway, the oak pews were restored one-by-one and refinished close to their original beauty. They were hard as a rock to sit on, requiring cushions, but beautiful as pews can be.

Once the pews were in place, the last furnishings were added, including draperies for the floor-to-ceiling glass-back walls, curtains for the window, wall sconces, hanging lanterns, an American flag and a pulpit.

What about sound?

Another can-do friend came to mind - Barry Lee.

Barry Lee, a professional sound man, installed a state-of-the-art sound system, complete with hidden speakers in the walls at the front and back of the sanctuary.

What about a video projector?

I had seen an amazing system at the south campus of Christ Fellowship on Northlake Boulevard. I spoke to Todd Mullins, the worship pastor, who later became senior pastor of Christ Fellowship. He kindly and graciously helped us install a video projector recessed in the ceiling with a drop-down recessed projection screen, all remotely operated from Barry Lee's sound booth.

With the sign "PARAMOUNT CHURCH," made by the Phil Rowe Sign Company and placed just outside the entrance-way of the sanctuary, we were ready.

One more thing.

We needed Bibles, imprinted with *Paramount Church,* for the slots in the back of the pews. Inspiration House handled that.

We were now ready to begin church services!

CHAPTER

72

Palm Beach, Florida

MY GOODNESS, I THOUGHT. PEOPLE ACTUALLY DID COME TO OUR FIRST CHURCH SERVICE.

It was August 24, 1994. A Sunday, of course.

I looked around the sanctuary, which a few months ago had no ceiling, no carpeting, no furniture, no hanging lantern lights, no wall sconces, no pews, no curtains, no cross, no sound system, no projection equipment, no baby grand Yamaha piano and no pulpit.

The previously termite-infested eighty-year-old oak pews looked pristine with their mahogany refinishing.

A "PARAMOUNT CHURCH" sign, just outside the entrance to the sanctuary, let it be known that suites 31 and 32 in the Paramount were now a church.

I thought, *only God could have accomplished the miraculous transformation of a dress design studio into a church sanctuary in a matter of months.*

Of course it was Gene Lawrence and Richard Moody who made it all happen.

And both provided all of their services for free!

I sent out special invitations for our first service to friends, family members, Bible study attendees, well-wishers and especially the thirty-one people who had endorsed the idea of coming to Palm Beach.

This was a daunting task. I knew that others had attempted to start churches in Palm Beach through the years, but none had continued after a few years. The last church to establish itself and remain was St. Edward Catholic Church in 1926. The Royal Poinciana Chapel began in 1898 and The Episcopal Church of Bethesda-by-the-Sea in 1925.

Would people come?

To my amazement, forty-five to fifty people came for that first service.

I spoke on the "Meaning of Life."

Why not?

That was what I had discovered when I opened my heart to God and invited Jesus into my heart. It was a meaning far beyond my previous professional career as a physician. And I had to share what I had discovered.

I had come from being an atheist, nineteen years previously, to a belief in the One True Almighty God of the Bible and in the Gospel of Jesus Christ. That led to my discovery of my true meaning, purpose and significance in the life that I had been given by God.

My long and winding road from medicine to ministry led me to the opening of the Paramount Church. In retrospect, there have been "nudges" along the way in which it seems that God had been orchestrating this path since 1967, and probably sooner.

CHAPTER

73

ONE NUDGE, AFTER ANOTHER, AFTER ANOTHER.

"... let us run with perseverance
the **race marked out for us.**"

HEBREWS 12:1

I came to believe that there actually was a *race marked out for me.* That was my conclusion. Too many things, in retrospect, made no sense unless there was a divine plan.

There have been *eleven nudges* in all.

All were life-changing decisions. Amazingly, the first five I experienced *before* I even believed in God.

The *first nudge* pointed me in the direction of medicine, which began in the summer of 1967 between my third and fourth year of college with the thought, "I'll volunteer in an emergency room." (Chapter 18)

There was nothing in my background to lead me in the direction of medicine.

Absolutely nothing!

This thought had to come from God. There is no other explanation.

The *second nudge* was a desire to experience general surgery and plastic surgery in the real world. I went to San Diego, where I met a dermatology resident at a New Year's Eve party who explained to me the medical subspecialty of dermatology. (Chapter 27)

The *third nudge* was the chief of dermatology at my medical school sending me to New York to experience dermatology.

(Chapters 30 & 31)

The *fourth nudge* was when I didn't match internships, leading me to apply for and be accepted in a new pilot program at NYU, a split dermatology/internal medicine internship. (Chapter 33)

The *fifth nudge* was being invited to join the Palm Beach Medical Group in West Palm Beach. (Chapter 37)

The *sixth nudge* was finding a church to attend from watching the LPGA Open Championship on television in 1985. The pastor of that church became my personal shepherd. (Chapters 45 & 46)

The *seventh* nudge was one day, out-of-the-blue, deciding to make a medical mission trip to Honduras. (Chapter 54)

The *eighth nudge* was retiring from private practice and offering my services to the Palm Beach County Health Department. (Chapters 60 & 61)

The *ninth nudge* was H. Loy Anderson, Jr. suggesting I come to Palm Beach to start a church. (Chapter 16)

The *tenth nudge* was Jim Partington suggesting I start the church in the Paramount in Palm Beach. (Chapter 25)

The *eleventh nudge* was a phone call, also out-of-the-blue, from the new owners of the Paramount, after initially being turned down by the previous owner, to start a church in the Paramount. (Chapter 50)

Each of these *nudges* definitely was not my thinking at the time.

In retrospect, they all had to be part of God's plan for my life, *the race marked out for me.*

The race marked out for me has essentially been in two parts. The first was becoming a medical doctor, practicing dermatology for fifteen years and then working in public health.

The second part has been founding and pastoring a church.

Neither were simple and straightforward. Both contained numerous twists and turns along the way.

Like everyone, my race has had its share of hardships, valleys, uphill climbs, roadblocks, crossroads, storms and impossible "Red Sea" impasses. I've experienced temptations to drop out of the race. I've experienced weariness and running alone with no one at my side. There were times in the wilderness and in the desert and times in the valley of the shadow of death, when all seemed hopeless.

There have been times when I had to step out in faith rather than by sight; times when I faced people who were "Goliaths" to me; times when it felt like I was in a "fiery furnace;" times when I had to ask for prayer; times when I had to ask God for strength and times when I had to ask for God's grace.

There also have been times when I had to acknowledge and admit my sin; times when I had to ask for forgiveness; times when I had to ask for help; times of great anguish like Jesus in the Garden of Gethsemane and times when I personally experienced the power of God.

All have been for my benefit and helped draw me closer to God.

These experiences helped to correct me, change me, alter my thinking, alter my behavior, alter my habits, make me more compassionate, make me kinder, make me more patient, make me more loving, make me more humble, make me less judgmental, make me more trusting and more dependent upon God and bring me to surrender even more.

The challenges along the way forced me to stand on God's Word, to enable me to better understand God, to make me more holy for God's purposes and to learn spiritual warfare.

Paul said to *know Christ* is to know the *fellowship of sharing in His sufferings* as well as the *power of His resurrection* (Philippians 3:10). Many of my hardships have given me a glimpse of the sufferings of Jesus Christ and a greater appreciation and better understanding of His sacrifice for me.

Like Paul, my desire is to finish the race that God has marked out for me.

> *"However, I consider my life worth nothing to me, if only I may **finish the race** and complete the task the Lord Jesus has given me ..."*

ACTS 20:24

74

GOD, YOU SURE HAVE A SENSE OF HUMOR.

Isn't it ironic that a dermatologist who works on people's outsides has been called to work on people's insides?

On the surface, it makes no sense!

But then it made no sense to call Moses to lead his people after he killed an Egyptian and gave God five, yes *five*, excuses why he thought God should use someone else.

It made no sense that an orphan girl, yes an orphan girl Esther, would save her people from annihilation.

It made no sense that Gideon, hiding in a wine press from the Midianites, would be addressed as a mighty warrior and lead his tiny army to victory when they were outnumbered 450 to 1.

It made no sense that Peter, a fisherman, someone who denied Christ three times, would become a great evangelist who led thousands to believe in Jesus Christ.

It made no sense that Saul, determined to wipe out the heretical sect of Jesus' followers, would become the great apostle Paul and author of half the New Testament.

It just made no sense for me, a dermatologist, to become a preacher of the Gospel of Jesus Christ and start a church in Palm Beach.

But God does things differently than one might expect. He even tells us that in Isaiah 55:8-9:

"For my thoughts are not your thoughts, neither are your ways my ways," declares the Lord. "As the heavens are higher than the earth, so are my ways higher than your ways and my thoughts than your thoughts."

It's no secret that God thinks and does things differently than we do.

We look at the outside. God looks at the inside (1 Samuel 16:7).

We love conditionally. God loves unconditionally.

And why me?

Why did God call me to found and pastor a church?

My doctorate in medicine doesn't qualify me to be a pastor.

My shortcomings are too many to count, my failings too many to list, my sinfulness too great to ignore and my mistakes too many to list. Like Moses, I could easily have given excuse after excuse why someone else should do what I do.

But I discovered that God isn't looking for perfect people. There aren't any. If there were perfect people, sinless people, there would be no need for Jesus.

After giving more than 1,000 Sunday sermons and 300 to 400 Bible teachings, there is always a knot in my stomach beforehand.

Each time I know I cannot inspire with my own words.

I am totally dependent upon the Holy Spirit to enable me to present a sermon or a teaching that truly represents God and His Bible.

Maybe God called me because He has personally proved Himself to me so many times in so many different ways that I have no doubt that He exists and that He is the One True God of the Bible.

Maybe because I am convinced that the Bible is God's Word, God's will, God's heart, God's thoughts and God's ways.

Maybe because I am persistent. The only way to get through medical school is to be persistent in the face of years of hardship and to stay the course no matter what.

Maybe because God has always been faithful when I was lacking the strength and the wisdom.

Maybe because I love Palm Beach and the people of Palm Beach.

Before starting the church in 1994, I practiced medicine for fifteen years and treated countless patients from Palm Beach. Many became friends. Many invited me into their homes in Palm Beach, in other states and some even in other countries.

But *why start another church … in Palm Beach?*

75

WHY PALM BEACH?

Almost everyone knows about Palm Beach, but not everyone knows *everything* about Palm Beach.

Every year, there are new *"Tell All"* books about Palm Beach, written by a "journalist" visitor or, occasionally, by a local resident. They all seem to focus on the external, very public, Palm Beach. It seems to sell books. Basically, they are mostly compilations of gossip.

Palm Beach is no secret.

It is known worldwide to the rich and famous, as well as to those who like to see and read about the rich and famous.

It has been a resort town for America's wealthy since its inception in the final decade of the nineteenth century. It's a veritable paradise, beckoning like a siren to the successful, to the famous, to the infamous … even to the wannabes.

Palm Beach is more than a location. It is a lifestyle of luxury, opulence and of elite fashionable society.

It is a town of extraordinary beauty, meticulous landscaping, balmy sunrises and sunsets, ubiquitous palm trees and a tranquility that makes one feel safe anytime of the day or night. And all this with a small town ambiance.

Oceanfront and lakefront palatial mansions and estates abound behind the hedges. Bentleys, Rolls-Royces and Lamborghinis are so common they are not given a second glance.

Palm Beach has its own history, with architectural treasures like the Breakers hotel, the Flagler Museum, Mar-a-Lago, the Vias of Worth Avenue, The Episcopal Church of Bethesda-by-the Sea and the Paramount Theater building. All are one-of-a-kind architectural jewels preserved in the style reflecting their origins between 1900 and 1927.

Residents are repeatedly members of The Forbes 400, always near the top and listed by name in the town newspaper the *Palm Beach Daily News,* also known as the "Shiny Sheet."

The "season," from early November to late April, swells the population from more than 8,000 year-round residents to 30,000. The season offers a never-ending assortment of social engagements. Galas, dinner parties, cocktail parties and private concerts are on tap during the season … always with the best food and wine.

Black tie and evening gowns are synonymous with the glamour and elegance that is Palm Beach.

Everyone who knows about Palm Beach is familiar with the opulence and grandeur.

As I have been a pastor of a Palm Beach church for the past twenty-two years and have lived on the island for most of that time, I can attest that all the above descriptions are accurate.

But that is not the *whole story* of today's Palm Beach.

There is one other little element, known only by word of mouth. It's something one will not find in travel brochures or through a Google search. There has been a shift of emphasis from the material to the spiritual for many.

An ever-increasing number of people feel a need to have God in their lives and feel a desire to understand the Bible. This includes both year-round residents and those who come for the "season."

What accounts for this?

There is enjoyment from all the pleasantries that Palm Beach offers. Yet I believe many have discovered that an earthly paradise, by itself, does not completely fulfill the yearnings of *the soul*.

Some have concluded that great successes and achievements have left them still wanting … something.

Could we have in Palm Beach a modern-day example of the Book of Ecclesiastes?

The author of Ecclesiastes, Solomon, was in the unique position as king of being able to indulge his every whim. He was able *to do ... to experience ... to accumulate ... everything and anything.*

Yet when all was said and done, he looked back and concluded it was *all meaningless, a chasing after the wind.*

He concluded that his life *only had meaning in serving and obeying God.*

Wealth can insulate from many of the trials of life, but, by itself, does not bring the deeper satisfaction that a personal relationship with God provides.

Wealth can be used for great philanthropic endeavors, but the giving of wealth alone doesn't bring a deep intimacy with God.

The Parable of the Pearl of Great Price in Matthew 13:45-46 is an illustration of the *true riches in life* coming not from material possessions, but from an understanding of the kingdom of God and the unsearchable riches of Christ.

There is no shop that sells the nine "fruit of the Spirit" listed in Galatians 5:22 ... love ... joy ... peace ... patience ... kindness ... goodness ... faithfulness ... gentleness ... self-control.

And there is no price tag on these transcendent attributes produced by the Holy Spirit.

They are free!

They are the true riches!

76

NOW WHAT?

How do I conclude this meandering saga of *Atheist Doctor To Palm Beach Minister?*

What I have learned in the past thirty-one years as a Christian is simple! There is a God and He is accessible through the atoning blood of Jesus Christ.

My story is as simple as the analogy of the man who spent his entire life climbing a ladder. When he arrived at the top of the ladder, he discovered his ladder was against the wrong building. My life as a successful professional medical doctor was great in many ways, but there was no God in my life and my goals were totally selfish.

My life had some meaning before I became a Christian, but it was not even close to the meaning my life has taken on since I became a Christian.

There are some wonderful people here on earth who I have met, but none give me the satisfaction that a personal relationship with God gives to me.

People will eventually disappoint in some fashion. God will never disappoint.

People can never really understand me. Only God can understand me.

People can never know me as God knows me.

The Bible is God's Word to us, not only for our lifetime but also for a history of mankind, which will, one day, end in a dramatic way.

My words of advice are simple and true ... ***turn your life over to God.***

How do you do that?

It takes two steps.

The first step is to invite Jesus into your heart and receive Jesus as God's gift for your salvation from your sinful nature. That will then enable you to begin to have a personal, intimate and practical relationship with God.

You may ask, how do I invite and receive Jesus into my heart?

It's very simple. Just earnestly, sincerely say this prayer:

"Jesus, thank you for going to the cross for me. I believe that you died for my sins and rose from the dead. Thank you for shedding your blood for me that I may be forgiven of my sins.

I invite you into my heart right now. I receive you, Jesus, as my own personal Savior and Lord. I give my life over to you. Lead me, guide me, teach me your plans and purposes for my life that I might bring glory and honor to you. I say this prayer by faith. In Jesus' Name, Amen."

If you said that prayer for the first time, you are about to embark on God's will for your life.

The journey will be an adventure.

And eternity with God is in store for you.

The second step is to plant yourself in a Bible-teaching, Bible-believing church that teaches and preaches the Gospel of Jesus Christ and teaches the Bible in a practical meaningful way. This sometimes is not so easy. Many churches don't teach or preach the Gospel of Jesus Christ or believe the Bible is God's heart and will to mankind. Search around until you find one that is right for you and become planted with a pastor to shepherd you personally. We all need a pastor. I do. You do.

Thank you for reading and may God bless you as only He can.

Thank you for reading my story.

Everyone is welcome to join us at our Sunday worship services 10:30 a.m. at the Paramount Church, 139 North County Road, Palm Beach, Florida. For further information, please call 561-835-0200.

The Historic Landmark Paramount Theater Photographic & Memorabilia Exhibit in the Paramount building is open to the public free of charge Monday through Friday 9 a.m. to 4 p.m.

Please visit our website at www.paramountchurchpb.com

Email: paramountchurchpb@gmail.com

INDEX

OLD TESTAMENT

Genesis 41:51-52, 282

1 Samuel 16:7, 305

Psalm 14:1, 11, 182

Psalm 28:2, 225

Psalm 34:18, 282

Psalm 53:1, 11, 182

Psalm 63:4, 225

Psalm 66:1, 226

Psalm 81:1, 226

Psalm 95:1, 226

Psalm 98:4, 226

Psalm 100:1, 226

Psalm 109:16, 282

Psalm 139:13-16, 76

Psalm 141:2, 225

Psalm 147:3, 282

Psalm 150, 224, 226

Isaiah 55:8-9, 305

Isaiah 61:1, 282

Isaiah 65:1, 184

Malachi 3:10, 252, 253

NEW TESTAMENT